STORIES FROM ADAM AND EVE TO EZEKIEL

# STORIES FROM ADAM AND EVE TO EZEKIEL

RETOLD FROM THE BIBLE BY

## CELIA BARKER LOTTRIDGE

ILLUSTRATED BY

## GARY CLEMENT

A **GROUNDWOOD BOOK** | DOUGLAS & McINTYRE
TORONTO  VANCOUVER  BERKELEY

Groundwood Books / Douglas & McIntyre
720 Bathurst Street, Suite 500, Toronto, Ontario M5S 2R4

Distributed in the USA by Publishers Group West
1700 Fourth Street, Berkeley, CA 94710

We acknowledge for their financial support of our publishing program the Canada Council
for the Arts, the Government of Canada through the Book Publishing Industry Development
Program (BPIDP), the Ontario Arts Council and the Government of Ontario through the
Ontario Media Development Corporation's Ontario Book Initiative.

ONTARIO ARTS COUNCIL
CONSEIL DES ARTS DE L'ONTARIO

National Library of Canada Cataloging in Publication
Lottridge, Celia B. (Celia Barker)
Stories from Adam and Eve to Ezekiel : retold from the Bible / by Celia Barker Lottridge;
illustrated by Gary Clement.
ISBN 0-88899-490-7
1. Bible stories, English. I. Clement, Gary II. Title.
BS551.3L67 2004     j220.9'505     C2003-907320-3

Design by Michael Solomon
Printed and bound in Canada

To Patsy Aldana and Michael Solomon
– CBL


To Gill, Sarah and Benjamin
– GC

# TABLE OF CONTENTS

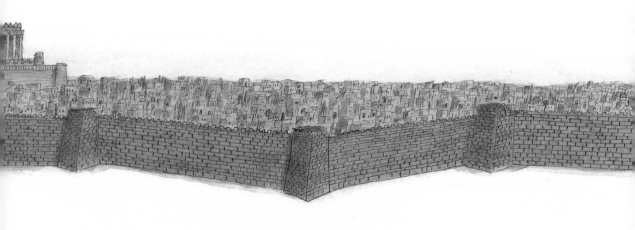

# FOREWORD

In this book you will find stories that start with the creation of the world and take you through the history of the people who became known as the Israelites. You will meet extraordinary individuals — Noah, Abraham, Miriam, Moses, Esther, Daniel — and come to know the circumstances of their lives and the challenges they met. These stories are retold from the Hebrew Bible, an ancient group of books that contain history, treatises on law, lists of the ancestors and descendants of important individuals, prophecy, poetry and the sayings of wise thinkers, all expressing the changing relationship of the Jewish people to God.

Woven through the history and the words of the prophets and poets are stories. They range from the poetic account of creation to celebrations of brave feats and great leaders. There are stories of terrible struggles that people go through as they heed or do not heed the word of God. There is trickery and conflict and tender love. Most of all there are people and moments you will not forget — Abraham leading his son, Isaac, up the mountain, thinking that he must sacrifice him; Miriam standing among the reeds of the Nile River, watching Pharaoh's daughter open a basket; young David running toward the giant Goliath, whirling his sling around his head.

All of the varied elements of the Hebrew Bible were written down by Jewish scribes, scholars, thinkers and students between the eleventh century B.C.E. and the second century B.C.E. Writing was highly valued during these centuries, but very few people actually knew how to write or read. Important stories, laws and poetry were learned and told or read aloud so that people could know their heritage. When those who could write heard stories and other teachings, they often wrote them down. This process of listening and recording went on for generations and resulted in many documents, long and short, written in Hebrew and containing the precious records, thoughts and literature of the Jewish people.

It took many years for these documents to be assembled into the books we are familiar with, such as Genesis and Exodus, Ruth and Jonah. These books were eventually brought together to make up the sacred scripture now often called the Hebrew Bible. It is not known who decided which writings should be included, but very early in the Common Era its final shape had emerged, and through the process of translation it has come to us. Over the centuries this great work has had a profound and lasting influence on the laws, customs and literature of the Western world.

Out of all the hundreds of meaningful and fascinating stories in the Hebrew Bible I have retold thirty-two. Together they give a sense of the history of the Israelites as they emerged as a people, began to know the land that had been given to them, struggled to understand what God wanted of them, suffered exile in Egypt, regained their heritage, became one nation, were again scattered and then saw the beginnings of coming together once more.

While it is true that these stories have existed in written form for a very long time, they also have the feel of stories that have been told over and over again. Imagine the desert people who have sat under the stars remembering the story of Joseph and his brothers; the women who have stirred a pot over the fire and told about Esau, who carelessly traded his birthright for a bowl of just such a delicious lentil stew; and all the children who have heard about the animals going into the ark two by two.

This is the flavor I have tried to give to my telling of these stories – the flavor of stories told and valued and passed on over a very long time. The stories are full of remarkable characters, crucial choices and unforgettable images. They deal with the relationship between humans and God, men and women, parents and children, and among siblings and within communities. They are truly stories to read and think about and share, as they have always been shared, by reading them aloud and telling them.

Celia Barker Lottridge

# THE STORY OF CREATION

Genesis 1.1-2.3.

IN THE BEGINNING, before God made the heavens and the earth, there was only darkness and deep water. Nothing had shape, not the earth nor the heavens. But the breath of God moved upon the water.

And God said, "Let there be light," and there was light. And God saw that the light was good and he divided it from the darkness. He called the light Day and the darkness Night. So there was the evening and there was the morning – the first day.

Then God said, "Let there be a firmament, an arch of heaven, and some of the waters shall lie under heaven and some above it. And it was so, and there was the evening and there was the morning – the second day.

Now God said, "Let the waters under heaven come together in one place and let dry land appear." And it was so. And God called the dry land Earth. The gathered waters he called Seas. And he said, "Let grass and other plants and fruit trees grow upon the earth, each bearing seeds so that its kind may grow again." And God saw that it was good. And there was the evening and there was the morning – the third day.

And God said, "Let there be lights in the heavens to divide the day from the night and to mark the passage of the days and the seasons and the years." He made two great lights, the greater to rule over the day and the lesser over the night, and he made stars. And he set them all in the heavens to shine upon the earth. And God saw that it was good. And there was the evening and there was the morning – the fourth day.

Then God said, "Let there be small creatures and great ones in the oceans and waters of the earth. And let there be birds flying over the earth and under heaven." And God looked and saw that it was good. He blessed the creatures and birds and said, "Be fruitful and multiply. Fill the waters and the air with your kind." And there was the evening and there was the morning – the fifth day.

God said, "Let the earth bring forth animals of all kinds, great and small, walking and creeping, fierce and timid." And he looked and saw that it was good.

And then, in his own image, God created man and woman. He blessed them and gave them all the creatures and all the plants that he had created so that they might care for them and prosper. And he said to them, "Be fruitful and multiply." And God looked over all that he had created and he saw that it was very good. And there was the evening and there was the morning – the sixth day.

And so the heavens and the earth and all that are in them were finished. And on the seventh day, God rested.

# ADAM AND EVE

Genesis 2.4-3.24. IN THE FIRST days of the world, God took dust from the ground and formed it into a human shape. Then he breathed the breath of life into the nostrils of the figure he had made and it became a living being, the first person in the world. God named him Adam.

Then God planted a garden in the east, in a place called Eden. The garden was full of beautiful trees bearing delicious fruit. The tree of life was in the garden, and in the very middle grew the tree of the knowledge of good and evil. God took Adam into the garden and showed him the plants that he had made and the river that flowed among them.

"Cultivate this garden and keep it well," said God. "The trees are here for your enjoyment and you may eat all the fruit you want, except for the fruit of the tree of knowledge which grows here, in the middle of the garden. That fruit is forbidden to you and if you eat it, you will die."

God watched Adam as he walked alone among the trees and God thought, "This man needs more than food to eat and beauty to enjoy. He needs companions." So God gathered up more dust and made animals and birds of all kinds and brought them to Adam.

"Name these creatures," said God, "for they will live with you in the garden."

Adam spent days giving names to the animals of the field and forest and the birds of the air. All of them lived together, at peace with one another.

But God was still keeping watch and he saw that no animal or bird could be an equal partner to the man. So God put Adam into a deep sleep and from his side took a little bone and from the bone God made a woman.

When Adam woke and saw the woman, he knew that she was the one who would be a true partner and helpmate to him, for they were made of the same bone and the same flesh. And he called the woman Eve, which means Giver of Life.

For a time Eve and Adam lived in the garden among all the animals and birds, eating the fruit that God had made for them. But one of the animals, the serpent, was crafty and watchful. He saw that the man and the woman never ate the fruit from the beautiful tree that grew in the middle of the garden.

One day he said to Eve, "Did God forbid you to eat some of the fruit in the garden?"

"We may eat the fruit of every tree except the one that stands in the middle, for God told us that if we eat that fruit or touch that tree, we will die."

"You will not die," said the serpent, "but you will change. You will see much more than you see now. Like God, you will know everything – both good and evil."

Eve believed the serpent and she thought, "Surely this

beautiful fruit will not harm us, and if our eyes are opened and we see good and evil, we will be wise."

And so when Eve was walking with Adam in the garden, she took one of the fruits of that tree and ate it. She gave some to Adam and he ate, too.

Then Eve and Adam looked at each other, and even though nothing had changed, what they saw looked different to them. Suddenly they felt ashamed because they were naked. They began to think, "We are living the way the animals live and we should not do that. We should cover our bodies." So they braided fig leaves together and made garments to wrap around themselves.

Then they heard the footsteps of God walking in the cool of the garden. For the first time Adam and Eve did not want to meet him because they knew that he would be angered by what they had done. Quickly, they hid among the trees. But God called to them and they had to come out from their hiding place. When he looked at them, he knew at once that they had eaten the fruit from the tree of knowledge.

"Why did you go against my command?" asked God.

"Eve gave the fruit to me," said Adam, "and I ate."

"It was the serpent," said Eve. "His deceitful words tempted me and I wanted to eat the fruit."

God turned to the serpent. "Because you have done this, you shall creep upon your belly and eat dust all the days of your life. Your children and the children of Eve will hate each other. They will strike you in the head and you will strike at their heels."

To Adam and Eve God said, "You have eaten fruit from the

tree of the knowledge of good and evil. Therefore you can no longer live in this garden where all you need is provided and where no harm will come to you. Your life here is over. You must go out into the world where you will know hardship and pain. You will labor and sweat to get food. Thistles will grow among the good grain in your fields. And in the end, you will return to the dust from which I made you."

And so Adam and Eve were sent out from the pleasant place they had known, out into the world with the knowledge of good and evil in their hearts.

And God placed a winged cherubim with a flaming sword at the gate to the garden so that they could never return.

# CAIN AND ABEL

ADAM AND EVE learned to live in the harsh land outside the garden of Eden, and in time they had two sons. The firstborn was called Cain and when he grew to be a man, he settled in one place and lived by planting and harvesting. His brother, Abel, was restless and became a keeper of sheep. He wandered the land following his flocks.

When their fields and flocks were well established, Cain and Abel brought offerings to the Lord, as was the custom. Cain brought grain and Abel brought the fattest of the first lambs from his flocks.

The Lord was pleased with Abel's offering, but Cain's offering did not please him. Cain was angry and disappointed and he showed it in his face.

God spoke to him and said, "There is no need for you to be angry. If you go and strive to do well, you will always be accepted. But jealousy and anger will only lead you into trouble."

But Cain kept his anger burning and turned it toward his brother. He said to Abel, "Come out into the field with me." When they had walked far and were alone, Cain struck his brother and killed him and left him there.

When he returned from the field, he heard God speaking to him.

"Where is your brother?"

"Why should I know?" said Cain. "Am I my brother's keeper? Must I always know where he is?"

"You know where he is," said God. "And I know, too. You have caused your brother's blood to fall on the ground. And I tell you that from this time onward, the ground will give you nothing. You will be a wanderer on the earth and will belong nowhere."

Cain cried out, "I cannot bear such punishment! I will have no fields to tend. I will be a fugitive and will never behold your face again. And anyone I meet may kill me."

"No," said God. "Being killed is not your punishment. I will put a mark upon you so that all who meet you will know who you are. If anyone kills you, that one will suffer a seven-fold punishment. Now, go."

And Cain went far away to the east, to the land of Nod on the other side of Eden. But wherever he went, people saw the mark God had put upon him and knew that he was Cain who had killed his brother.

But Adam and Eve were not left without sons. Eve gave birth to Seth and Seth had many descendants.

# NOAH AND THE FLOOD

Genesis 6.5-9.17. AFTER THE TIME of Adam and Eve and their children many generations passed. With every generation there were more people, and with every generation it seemed that the people grew farther and farther away from God. At last there was so much wickedness in their hearts that God looked at the world and saw nothing but meanness and cruelty and violence.

"I am sorry that I created these people, for they do nothing but harm," said God. "I will blot them out. I will destroy all the life I have created."

But then God remembered Noah. Noah was a good man. He had not forgotten God, and he lived as righteously as he could in the wicked world. And Noah had a wife and three sons, Shem, Ham and Japheth, and each son had a wife.

God made a plan and told it to Noah.

"In seven days I will send a great flood to wash away all the evil and violence in the world. I will open the windows of heaven and it will rain for forty days and forty nights and all the fountains of the deep will burst forth. Every creature that draws the breath of life will be destroyed. But the world should not end, and you will help me save the good that is there to save.

"Noah, hear me! Build a great boat, an ark, out of cypress wood. Make it one hundred and fifty paces long, twenty-five paces wide and taller than the tallest cypress tree. You must build three decks and many rooms within the ark and put a great door in the side. And near the top make a window that will open.

"When the ark is built, bring your wife, your sons and your sons' wives into it. And you must bring two of every animal, male and female, into the ark. Two of each kind of bird and beast and creeping thing that lives upon the earth. And you must bring food of every kind so that all may eat until the waters of the flood are gone."

Noah believed the words of God. With the help of his sons he built the ark just as he had been commanded. It stood tall and strong upon the dry earth. When it was ready, the beasts and the birds and the creeping things came, two by two, through the open door and all found their places.

The rain began just as Noah was closing the door behind the last of the creatures. Soon water covered the land and the ark began to float. The rain fell without stopping, and the water rose and rose until all the high mountains under heaven were covered.

And it rained for forty days and forty nights.

But God remembered Noah and his family and all the animals, and at last he stopped the rain. Then he made the wind blow and the waters began to recede. On the seventeenth day of the seventh month, the ark stopped drifting upon the water. It came to rest on the mountain of Ararat. Noah looked out of the high window but all he could see was water stretching away in every direction.

So he opened the window and sent forth a raven. The great black bird flew to and fro over the water, but at last it returned to Noah. It had found no dry land. After seven days Noah sent out a dove, but the dove, too, found no place to set its foot and returned to the ark.

Noah waited seven more days and sent the dove out again. This time the dove was gone for many days, but at last it returned. It lit on Noah's outstretched hand and he saw that in its beak, it held an olive leaf. Then Noah knew that somewhere trees rose above the waters and were sending forth new leaves. After seven days he sent the dove out once more. This time it did not return.

Noah called his family together and they opened the great door in the side of the ark and looked out. They saw no water, only damp earth, and they rejoiced.

God said to Noah, "Go out of the ark, you and your wife and your sons and their wives. Bring out all the living things so that they may abound on the earth and multiply."

The first thing Noah and his family did when they set their feet upon dry ground was to build an altar and give thanks to God.

God was pleased. He said in his heart, "The humans I have created cannot help doing wrong things sometimes. It is part of their nature and it will always cause trouble. But I will never again curse the earth because of it. I will not destroy all the wonderful life that I have created."

Then God spoke to Noah, "I give you this promise. I will never again send a flood to cover the earth. From now on, seedtime and harvest, cold winter and hot summer, day and night will not end as long as the earth endures."

And God put a rainbow in the sky and spoke again. "This is a sign. When you see a rainbow you will know that I am remembering my promise to you and all people."

Then Noah and his wife with Shem, Ham, Japheth and their wives began to cultivate the earth once more.

# THE TOWER OF BABEL

Genesis 11.1-9.28.

FOR A LONG TIME after the great flood, all the people on earth spoke the same language. They migrated from the east, living in tents and following their flocks of sheep and goats, always seeking new pastures.

After many years they came to a wide plain in the land of Shinar where great rivers flowed. Perhaps they were tired of wandering, for when they found clay in the riverbanks, they shaped it into bricks, which they baked in hot fires to make them strong.

With the bricks they could build houses to live in. And in time they had built so many houses that they had created a city, which came to be known as Babel. And then they built a great wall to protect the city.

The people were pleased with their city and proud of their skill in building. They had all of the houses and shops and stables that they needed, so they began to think of building something for glory and not for use.

"We will build a tower," they said. "A tower so high that its top will reach heaven. A tower so great that it can be seen from afar. We will know that we belong in the shadow of the tower, and we will not scatter over the face of the whole earth.

And whoever sees our tower will know that we are a great and powerful people." And so they began to build.

Now, as the builders worked and the tower grew higher and higher, God noticed that it was reaching toward heaven. He came down to see what the people were doing. They did not know him as he walked among them and watched them forming bricks, baking them and carrying them up long ladders to the top of the tower, already high in the clouds. He saw that these people would not stop. They would build a tower to heaven.

"And that is only the beginning of what they might do," God thought. "They are one people and they have one language. And they do not understand that they should not build a tower as high as heaven."

And so God thought of a way to make it impossible for the people to work together with all their skill and strength to build one structure that would stand alone in all the world.

He came again to the city and this time, as he passed among the people, they forgot the language they had always spoken. Each one began to speak a different new language, one that had never been spoken before.

Now the people could not understand each other. They could not work together. They could not even remember why they wanted to build a tower. So they put down their tools and wandered away from the tower and the city. They scattered abroad over the face of the earth, and each began to build and live in a new way.

And the tower of Babel stood alone and unfinished with only God to look at it, from heaven.

# GOD SPEAKS TO ABRAHAM

Genesis 12.1-10,
13.14-18, 15.1-6,
18.1-14, 21.1-6.

ABRAHAM LIVED with his wife, Sarah, in the land of Haran. They had many relatives and were rich in possessions and servants. Abraham and Sarah's only sorrow was that they had no children.

One day Abraham was amazed to hear the voice of God speaking to him.

"Go from Haran," said God. "Leave your father's house and go to the land I will show you. You shall be the beginning of a great nation."

Abraham did not understand what these words could mean. How could he be the beginning of a great nation? He and Sarah were both old and they had no sons or daughters to carry on their family. But he was certain that he had heard God speak, and so he began to prepare his household for a great journey.

He gathered his slaves and servants, flocks of sheep and goats, cooking vessels and dishes, tents and blankets. When all was ready, Abraham and Sarah with all their household travelled south into the land of Canaan.

They came to a town called Shechem, to the oak of Moreh. There God appeared to Abraham and said, "I will give this land to your descendants." Again Abraham was puzzled but he believed that God would somehow keep his promise.

In Canaan, life was hard for Abraham's people. There was a drought in the land and they had to travel from one water hole to another to find food and water. For a time they went down into Egypt where the Nile River made the fields green even in dry years.

At last Abraham began to prosper. His flocks of sheep and goats grew. There was plenty of food for everyone. They were able to stop wandering and return to the hills of Canaan and pitch their tents near the place where Abraham had seen God.

Now God spoke again. "Look, Abraham," he said. "Look to the north, the south, the east and the west. All the land you see will be yours, and you will have offspring as countless as the grains of dust on the earth. Go and walk the length and breadth of this land, for I give it to you."

Still Abraham could not understand this promise. "How will this land belong to my offspring?" he wondered. "God has given me no children." And Sarah wondered, too.

One day as Abraham sat in the shade outside his tent, he saw three strangers standing nearby. He was surprised, for he had not seen them coming, but he ran to them and bowed and offered them the hospitality that desert people always gave to strangers.

"I am your servant," he said. "Let me have water brought so that you may wash your feet, for the day is hot and the way is dusty. Rest yourselves under the tree and eat a little bread. Then you may go on your way refreshed."

He called to a servant for water and then rushed to Sarah and said, "Quickly! Make cakes of the best flour and I will

have a calf killed and meat roasted, for I am sure that these guests should be honored."

All of this was done and the food was set before the strangers. As they ate, one of them said to Abraham, "Where is your wife, Sarah?"

"She is in the tent," said Abraham, wondering how they knew of Sarah.

The strangers looked toward the door of the tent and said, "In due season Sarah shall bear a son."

Sarah heard these words. For a moment she thought, "Maybe it could be true." Then she laughed to herself, for how could anyone think that this joy could come to her now that she was old.

But Abraham said nothing, for he was sure that these were messengers from God.

And the stranger said, "Why did Sarah laugh? Is anything too wonderful for God? I promise you, Sarah will have a son."

And indeed, Sarah and Abraham had a son. He was a fine, strong boy and they called him Isaac, which in Hebrew sounds like the word for laughter. For Sarah said, "I laughed with wonder when I thought of having this child. Now God has made me laugh with joy. May everyone feel my joy and laugh with me."

# SODOM AND GOMORRAH

Genesis 18.16-33, 19.1-29. THE TWO CITIES of Sodom and Gomorrah lay in the fertile valley of the Jordan River. The cities were prosperous but they were filled with wicked people who lived wild lives and hated strangers. The one good man in Sodom was Lot, the nephew of Abraham. He and his family lived as they believed God wished them to.

God heard about the wickedness of the two cities and when he went with two angels, in the guise of travelers, to tell Abraham and Sarah that they would have a son, he decided to send the angels on to see whether the reports were true.

Abraham walked with the three travelers as they left his tents, to set them on the way to Sodom. Suddenly one of the travelers turned to Abraham and spoke in a voice that Abraham had heard before. He knew that it was the voice of God.

"These two will go to Sodom and if I learn that the people there are as wicked as I have heard, that city and the city of Gomorrah will be destroyed," he said. And he sent the two angels on their way.

Abraham stood before the Lord. He thought of Lot and his family. They did not deserve to be destroyed. Perhaps there were others like them in Sodom.

"O Lord," he said. "You are a just God. Surely you will not destroy those who are not wicked. What if there are fifty righteous people in Sodom? Will you not spare the city for their sake?"

"Yes," said God. "If there are fifty righteous people, I will not destroy the city."

"What if there are five fewer righteous people? Will you then spare the city?"

"Yes," said God. "For forty-five good people, I will not destroy Sodom."

Abraham knew that in Lot's family there were only four, so he said, "I am worth no more than dust and ashes, but I take it upon myself to speak to the Lord. For forty righteous people would you spare the city?"

"Yes," said the Lord.

"And for thirty? Or twenty? Or even ten?"

"If there are ten in Sodom who honor me and live as they should, I will not destroy the city." Then the Lord was gone and Abraham went back to his tent.

When the two angels whom the Lord had sent arrived in Sodom, they found Lot sitting by the city gate. He bowed before them and said, "You are strangers in this place. Come to my house. I will be honored to welcome you with a meal and a place to sleep."

"There is no need," said one of the travelers. "We can sleep in the marketplace."

"It would not be safe," said Lot. "Come with me."

So the strangers went with Lot. They were given water to wash their feet and soon sat down to a good meal. As they ate they began to hear the noise of people gathering in the street outside the front door. All of the men of Sodom, young and old, were there. They began to shout, "Give us the strangers, Lot. We will show them that we do not like outsiders. Let us do to them what we will."

Lot went out and spoke to the men of Sodom.

"Brothers," he said, "do not act so wickedly. These men are guests in my house. I will not give them to you."

Someone shouted, "You came here from far away. You are an outsider yourself, yet you dare to judge us." And the crowd pressed against Lot and raised their fists against him. They pushed toward the door, hoping to break it down.

Suddenly the travelers flung the door open. They pulled Lot inside and gazed for a moment at the faces in the mob, ugly with anger. Then they closed the door.

Outside in the street the crowd was suddenly silent. Men blinked and rubbed their eyes. They wanted to smash the door down but they could not see it. Suddenly every one of them was blind. In a panic they began to push each other in all directions, trying to get away from Lot's house and from his powerful guests.

Lot and his family stared at the travelers. Now they could see that these were not ordinary men. Perhaps they were angels. Certainly they had been sent by God.

One of the travelers spoke. "You must leave Sodom at once. This city and Gomorrah will be destroyed because of the wickedness of the people. Only you will be saved. You must flee, and as you flee, you must not look back at the city or you will share its fate."

But Lot and his family could not seem to move. They were stunned by what they had heard. At last the travelers took them by their hands and led them out of the city.

"Go now," they said. "Do not look back."

Then the Lord sent a rain of sulfur and fire upon the two cities and upon the crops growing in the fields around them.

As Lot and his family walked away from Sodom, they could hear the crashing of buildings falling and see the light of flames in the sky. Lot remembered the words of the travelers and kept on walking. But his wife, hardly believing that what she was seeing and hearing could be true, forgot the warning and turned around. Immediately she was gone, and in her place stood a pillar of rock that glistened like crystals of salt in the red light of the burning city.

In the morning Abraham went to the place where he had spoken with the Lord. He looked toward the valley of the Jordan River and he could see thick smoke rising up into the sky. He knew that Sodom and Gomorrah had been destroyed.

But Lot was safe in the city of Zoar because God remembered Abraham and did not destroy the righteous.

# ABRAHAM AND ISAAC

ISAAC GREW and was truly the joy of his mother, Sarah, Genesis 22.1-19. and his father, Abraham. They believed that their son fulfilled God's promise that the land of Canaan would belong to their children and their children's children.

But God tested Abraham once more. In those days it was the custom for people to show their devotion to God by offering sacrifices of fine sheep and goats. Abraham often made such sacrifices. But this time God said, "Abraham, take your son, Isaac, your only son whom you love, and go to the land of Moriah and offer him there as a sacrifice to me. I will show you the place."

Abraham remembered the promise that God had made, that his descendants would people the earth. Surely Isaac was part of that promise. Yet now God said that he must be offered as a sacrifice. How could this be?

But Abraham had always obeyed the voice of God, and he believed that God's promises would always be kept. So he rose early in the morning, called for his young son and two servants, saddled his donkey and set out. They traveled for three days to a mountain in the land of Moriah.

Then Abraham said to the servants, "Stay here with the

donkey. Isaac and I will go up the mountain to worship and then come back to you."

He gave Isaac wood to carry and he himself carried his knife and a charcoal brazier full of fire. Together he and Isaac climbed up the mountain.

At last Isaac said, "Father, we have fire and wood, but where is the lamb for the offering?"

"God will provide the lamb," answered Abraham, and they walked on.

When they came to the place that God showed him, Abraham built an altar and laid the wood upon it. Then he bound Isaac and laid him on top of the wood. He waited a moment and then picked up his knife. Before he could lower it, he heard a voice from heaven.

"Abraham! Abraham!"

"Here I am," said Abraham.

"Do not harm the boy," said God. "I know now that you trust in me and fear me since you have been willing to give even your only son to me."

Then Abraham looked up and saw a ram caught in a thicket by its horns. He knew that the ram was the proper offering. So he freed Isaac and offered the ram to God.

Then the voice called from heaven again, "Because you have done this, I will indeed bless you. Your offspring will be as numerous as the stars in the heavens and as the sand on the seashore."

And then Abraham and Isaac went back down the mountain and journeyed home to Sarah.

# REBEKAH AT THE WELL

Genesis 24.1-67. WHEN ISAAC WAS GROWN, his father, Abraham, called his oldest servant and said, "Go to Haran where my family dwells, and bring back a wife for my son."

The servant said, "Perhaps no woman will be willing to leave her own land to marry Isaac, for she will not know him. May I take Isaac with me?"

"No," said Abraham. "Do not take my son with you, for when God took me from my father's house and the land of my birth, he promised the land of Canaan to me and to my descendants. Isaac must remain in Canaan. But God will send an angel to guide you, and if it should happen that the woman you find in Haran is not willing to come to Isaac, you will be released from your obligation."

And the servant swore that he would do as Abraham asked. Then he took ten of his master's camels and some men to accompany him and journeyed to the city where Abraham's brother Nahor dwelt.

It was evening when he arrived, the hour of the day when women would come to the well just outside the city to draw water. He took his camels to the well and made them kneel there, as camels do when they are resting. Then he prayed that

God would give him success and show kindness to his master, Abraham.

"I will speak to a young woman who comes to the well," he prayed. "If she offers me water from her pitcher and also draws water for my camels, let this be a sign that she is the one you have chosen for your servant Isaac."

Before he had finished praying he saw a young woman coming toward the well. She was very beautiful and carried a water pitcher on her shoulder. She went down to the well, lifted the pitcher from her shoulder and filled it. The servant ran to meet her as she walked up the slope with the filled pitcher.

"Please," he said, "let me drink a little water from your pitcher."

"Drink, my lord," she said, and lowered the pitcher so he could drink. "I will draw water for your camels also." She emptied her pitcher into the trough and then drew water until all the camels had drunk.

The servant stood quietly until he was sure that the angel had sent him the sign he had prayed for. When he saw that the camels had drunk their fill of water, he took out gifts he had brought – a gold nose ring and two gold bracelets.

"Is there room in your father's house for me to lodge while I am in this city?" he asked.

"We have room for you," she said, "and straw and feed enough for your camels."

"Whose daughter are you?" he asked.

"I am Rebekah, the daughter of Bethuel, the son of Milcah and Nahor."

The servant bowed his head and worshiped the Lord, for the angel had led him to the house of Abraham's kin. And he gave Rebekah the gifts.

Rebekah ran and told her mother and all her family about the man and his words and the gifts. Her brother Laban, seeing the nose ring and the bracelets, went to the man at the well and said, "Why do you stand here? The house is prepared for you and I have a place for the camels."

So Abraham's servant went into the house. He and the others with him were given water to wash their feet and food was set before them.

But the servant said, "I will not eat until I have delivered my message. I am the servant of Abraham, brother of Nahor. The Lord has greatly blessed my master with flocks and herds, silver and gold, donkeys and camels and slaves. All this Abraham has given to his son, Isaac. Now he has sent me to the land of his kinsfolk to seek a wife for his son. And so I have come. I prayed to the Lord for a sign, and the sign has been given that Rebekah, of this house, is the woman intended to be the wife of Isaac. Tell me now whether you will keep the faith of my master. If not, say so, and I will turn elsewhere."

And Rebekah's father and brother said, "Here is Rebekah. She will be the wife of Isaac as the Lord has decreed."

When the servant heard this he gave great thanks to the Lord. Then he brought out gold and silver ornaments and robes and gave them to Rebekah, and presented other costly gifts to her mother and brother.

In the morning the servant said, "Give me leave to take Rebekah and return to my master."

STORIES FROM ADAM AND EVE TO EZEKIEL

But her mother and brother said, "Let her stay with us a little, perhaps ten days, and then she shall go."

"I wish to tell my master without delay of the success the Lord has granted me," said the servant. "Do not detain me."

They said, "Let us call Rebekah and see what she says."

And Rebekah said, "I will go now."

So Rebekah and her nurse made ready to set out with Abraham's servant and his men. Her family blessed her, saying, "You are our sister. May you be the mother of myriads. May your offspring possess the gates of their enemies."

Then Rebekah and her companions mounted their camels and followed Abraham's servant into Canaan.

Isaac was waiting anxiously to know whether the servant would bring back a woman to be his wife. He brought his tents out into the open country of the Negeb, hoping to meet them. One evening, he walked beyond the camp and saw camels coming.

Rebekah was looking, too, as she rode among the others. She saw Isaac walking across the fields toward them and slipped hastily from her camel.

"Who is that man?" she asked.

"It is my master, Isaac," said the servant.

So she took her veil and covered her face while the servant told Isaac all that had happened.

Then Isaac brought Rebekah to his mother, Sarah, in her tent. And Rebekah became Isaac's wife and he loved her.

# JACOB AND ESAU

ISAAC PRAYED to the Lord because he and his wife, Rebekah, had no children. God heard the prayer and Rebekah became pregnant. But as she waited for her child to be born, it seemed to her that there was more than one child in her womb and that they were struggling with one another. Rebekah consulted with the Lord and said, "What is happening and what does it mean?"

Genesis 25.21-34.

The Lord said, "There are two children in your womb and they will grow up to lead two nations. One child will be stronger than the other and the elder will serve the younger. Already they have begun to contend with each other."

In the proper time Rebekah gave birth to twin sons. The firstborn was covered with a coat of soft reddish hair. He was named Esau, which means hairy. His brother came after him with his hand gripping Esau's heel. He was called Jacob, which means heel holder. They were twins, but Esau was the elder so he would one day be leader of the family and have double the inheritance of Jacob, his younger brother.

When the boys grew to be men, Esau became a skillful hunter who loved ranging over the fields in search of game. Jacob was a quiet man and stayed among the tents where his parents and their people lived. Isaac was most fond of Esau because he loved the taste of the wild game his elder son brought in. But Rebekah loved Jacob best.

One day Jacob was cooking a pot of red lentil stew when Esau came in from the fields. He was famished.

"Quick," he said. "Give me some of that red stew to eat. I am weak with hunger."

Jacob said, "If I give you some of this pottage you must give me all that will come to you as eldest son. You must sell me your birthright."

"Hah," said Esau. "What good is a birthright to me if I am dead from hunger?"

"Swear that you will sell it to me," said Jacob, "and then I will give you some stew."

And Esau swore that he would sell his birthright to his younger brother for a bowl of the pottage that smelled so good.

Then Jacob gave him bread and as much lentil stew as he wanted. Esau ate and drank and went on his way.

And that is how little Esau thought of his birthright.

# ISAAC BLESSES HIS SON

Genesis 27.1-45,
28.1-5.

ISAAC WAS OLD and he could no longer see. He felt that the day of his death might be near, and before he died he wanted to be sure to give his blessing to his favorite son, Esau.

He said to Esau, "Get your bow and quiver and hunt some wild game. Cook it the well-flavored way that I like and bring it to me. I will eat it and then I will give you my heart's blessing before I die."

So Esau took his bow and quiver and went hunting.

But Rebekah heard what Isaac said. She wanted the blessing to go to Jacob, who was her favorite son, so she said to him, "Your brother has gone to hunt game. He will cook it for your father. After Isaac eats he will give Esau his blessing. Now, do as I say and your father's blessing will be yours. Go out to the herd and bring me two fine young goats. I will cook the meat with the seasonings that Isaac likes, and you will take it to him. He will think that you are Esau. He will eat and then you will receive his blessing."

Jacob said, "But my brother Esau is a hairy man. My skin is smooth. If my father touches me, he will know that I have tricked him and I will receive his curses, not his blessing."

"If there is a curse, let it fall on me," said Rebekah. "Go and get the goats."

So Jacob brought the goats to his mother, and she prepared them in the way that Isaac loved. Then she fetched Esau's favorite clothes and told Jacob to put them on, and she covered his arms and his neck with the skins from the young goats.

"Now take the food to your father," she said.

Jacob went to Isaac and said, "Father, I have brought you the game you wanted. Sit up and eat and then give me your heart's blessing."

"You have been very quick, my son," said Isaac. "Come near so that I can touch you and be sure that you are Esau."

Jacob came to his father and Isaac touched him on the arm where Rebekah had placed the goat skin. It felt like Esau's arm but the voice was more like Jacob's.

"Are you really my older son?" Isaac asked.

Jacob said, "I am."

"Then bring the meat from the hunt," said Isaac. "I will eat it and give you my heart's blessing."

Jacob gave his father the food and he poured wine for him to drink.

When Isaac had eaten and drunk he said, "Come here, my son, and kiss me." And when Isaac kissed him, he breathed in the smell of the clothes Jacob was wearing, and they were Esau's clothes.

"Ah," said Isaac. "You smell of the fields the Lord has blessed. My son, may God give you the dew of heaven and plenty of grain and wine from the earth. I make you lord over your brothers, and nations shall bow down before you. A curse upon those who curse you and a blessing on those who bless you."

Isaac finished the blessing and Jacob left him. No sooner had he gone than Esau came in from his hunting. He immediately prepared the savory dish his father loved and brought it to him.

"Sit up, Father," he said, "and eat the meat I have brought from the hunt and give me your heart's blessing."

His father said, "Who are you?"

"I am Esau, you firstborn son."

Isaac began to tremble. "Who brought me meat before you came? I ate it and gave him my blessing, and I cannot take a blessing back."

Esau cried out loudly, "Father, bless me, too!"

"I cannot," said Isaac. "Your brother has tricked me and he has my blessing. He has cheated you."

"He deserves his name," said Esau. "He is a heel holder and grabs hold of what is mine, first my birthright and now my blessing. Is there no blessing left for me?"

Isaac said, "I have made him lord over you. I have given him the richness of the fields, grain and wine. I cannot give these things to you. You will live by the sword and serve your brother, but in time you will break loose and free yourself from him."

From that day on Esau hated Jacob. He said, "The time will come soon when we will mourn for my father. When the days of mourning are over, I will kill my brother."

Rebekah was told of Esau's words and she said to Jacob, "Your brother is comforting himself by planning to kill you. You must go to my brother Laban. Stay with him until Esau's anger cools. Then I will send you word and you can come home."

She went to Isaac and said, "I am afraid that Jacob will marry one of the Canaanite women instead of one of his own people. How can we save him from such an error?"

"I will take care of it," said Isaac.

He called Jacob to him and said, "Go east to Haran where your uncle Laban lives, and seek a wife among his daughters." And he asked the blessing of God upon his son.

And so Jacob set off for his uncle's house, fleeing his brother's anger and hoping to find a wife.

# JACOB'S LADDER

As Jacob traveled from Beersheba in Canaan to Genesis 28.10-22. Haran, he came to a desert place where many boulders were scattered on the ground. Darkness was coming on, so he chose a long flat stone to use for a pillow and lay down to sleep.

While he slept he had a wonderful dream. He dreamed that he saw a ladder reaching from the earth up into heaven, and angels of the Lord were going down the ladder and up again. God came and stood beside Jacob and said, "I am the Lord, God of Abraham and Isaac. I will give the land where you lie to you and your children and their children's children. Your descendants shall be as countless as the dust of the earth and shall spread to the west and to the east and to the north and to the south. I will protect you and bring you back to this land, and I will not leave you until I have done all that I have promised."

Jacob awoke. He looked around him and said, "Truly the Lord is in this place and I did not know it." He was filled with awe, for he knew that he was in the house of God, at the very gate of heaven.

When the sun rose, Jacob took the stone he had put under his head and set it upright as a sacred pillar. From his pack he

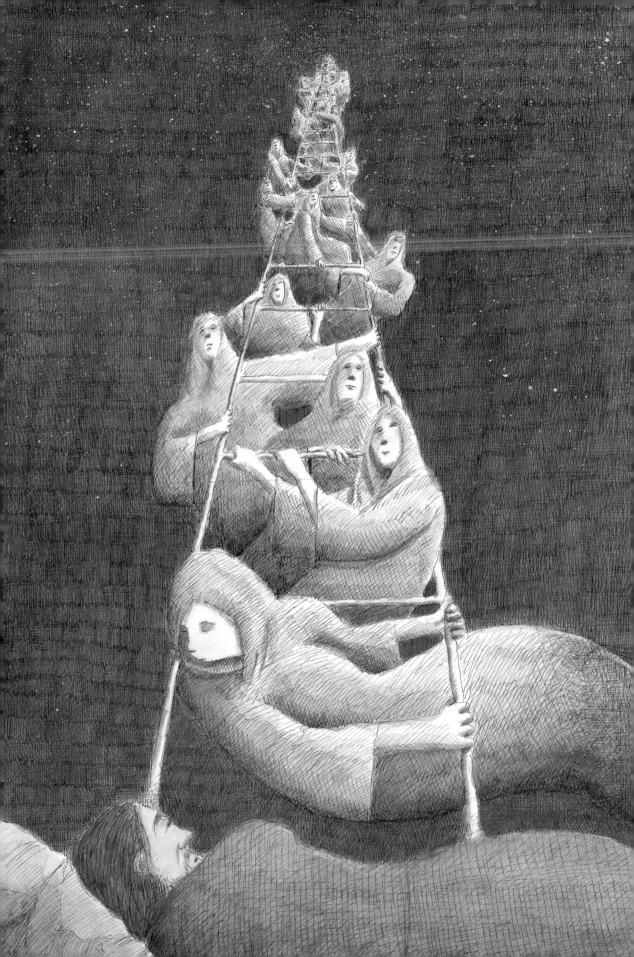

took a jar of oil and poured it on top of the pillar as an offering to the Lord.

Then Jacob made a vow, "If God will be with me and give me food to eat and clothes to wear and help me return to my father's house in peace, then I will come back to this place and build an altar to him."

And he named the place Bethel, which means House of God.

# JACOB AND LABAN

Genesis 29.1-30,
30.25-43, 31.1-55.

WHEN JACOB CAME to Haran he stopped to talk with some shepherds who were gathered at a well to water their sheep. He asked them whether they knew Laban, his uncle.

"We do," they replied. "And here is his daughter Rachel who tends her father's flocks."

When Rachel realized who Jacob was, she greeted him gladly. Then she ran and told her father that his kinsman had come and Laban, too, greeted Jacob with joy.

Jacob stayed for a month, doing work that would be useful to his uncle. Then Laban said to him, "You shouldn't work for me for nothing just because you are my nephew. Tell me, what wages should I pay you?"

Now Laban had two daughters. The elder was Leah but Jacob loved Rachel, the younger sister. He said, "I will work for you for seven years so that I may have Rachel for my wife." And Laban agreed.

So Jacob worked for seven years, but they seemed to him to be only a few days because of the great love he had for Rachel.

At the end of the seven years, Laban made a great feast and he gave Jacob his bride. As was the custom, she was wearing a

heavy veil. It was not until the morning after the feast that Jacob knew he had married his older cousin, Leah, not his beloved Rachel.

In anger he asked Laban, "Why have you deceived me? You know that I worked seven years for Rachel."

Laban said, "It is not done in our country to give the younger sister in marriage before the firstborn. But you don't have to wait to marry Rachel. You can marry her in a week if you promise to work for me for seven more years."

At that time many men had more than one wife, so Jacob agreed. He married Rachel and he worked for seven more years for Laban.

In time Jacob had the blessing of eleven sons but he still had little wealth, for all of the sheep and goats he cared for belonged to Laban. He decided that it was time for him to return to his own country with his wives and children.

But Laban did not want him to go. He knew that the Lord had been good to him for Jacob's sake and had made him prosperous with great flocks of sheep and goats. He said to Jacob, "I will pay you whatever you think is right. Only stay."

But Jacob did not trust Laban to be fair with him, so he said, "Give me no wages. Just agree to let me have the sheep and goats that are speckled in color. There are only a few, and if a sheep or a goat in my possession is not speckled, you will know that I have stolen it from you."

"Very well," said Laban.

And that very day, Jacob separated out the animals that were speckled and kept them away from Laban's sheep and goats. But it happened that both Laban's animals and Jacob's began bearing speckled kids and lambs, and they were healthy and strong. According to the agreement all the speckled beasts belonged to Jacob, and so Jacob's flocks grew and he also became rich in servants and camels and donkeys.

Some time passed and Jacob heard that the sons of Laban were saying that he was taking what was rightly theirs to make himself rich. He also saw that Laban was growing less favorable toward him. One day he asked Rachel and Leah to come with him to a distant field where his flocks were. He knew that no one would overhear them talking there.

Jacob said, "You know that I have served your father with all my strength, but he has tricked me and cheated me. It is God who has helped me. He has seen to it that many speckled animals are born, and so I have grown prosperous. But Laban is angry with me. And I must tell you that the angel of God called to me in a dream and said, "Leave this land. Go back to your own people.""

Rachel and Leah said, "Our father does not share his wealth with us. He sold us and we have received no benefit from the labor you paid. God is watching over us and our children. Do as God says."

Jacob said nothing to Laban. He gathered his servants, put his children and his wives on camels and loaded his possessions on donkeys. They all set out for the land of Canaan, driving the herds ahead of them.

When they had been gone three days, Laban realized that Jacob had fled with his family and flocks. He took his kinfolk and pursued Jacob into the hills of Gilead where he had set up his tents.

Then God came to Laban in a dream and said, "Let Jacob alone. Say nothing to him."

But Laban caught up with Jacob and said, "How could you steal away my daughters like captives of war? You did not even let me kiss my grandchildren and my daughters goodbye. I would have sent you off with singing and the sound of tambourines and harps. You have been foolish and I have it in my power to hurt you, but last night the God of your father spoke to me in a dream and said, 'Let Jacob alone.' So if you want to leave, go."

Now Jacob was angry. "I have served you these twenty years and your flocks have prospered. I have served in the cold and the heat. You have demanded payment from me if a beast was missing, yet I have never eaten one ram belonging to your flocks. You have paid me as it suited you. And now it is only because of my father's God that you will let me go."

Laban still said, "These women are my daughters, your children are my grandchildren, the sheep are my sheep. But there is nothing I can do. Let us make a covenant between us with the Lord as our witness. You can go, but you must treat my daughters well. If you mistreat them, remember, God is our witness."

And Jacob took the oath and made an offering to God. Then he called all the kinfolk to a feast and they slept that night on the hills. In the morning, Laban kissed his grandchildren and his daughters and blessed them and returned home.

# JACOB RETURNS
# TO CANAAN

Genesis 32.3-32,
33.1-14, 35.1-29.

JACOB SENT MESSENGERS to his brother, Esau, saying, "I, your brother, Jacob, am returning to Canaan after twenty years with our uncle Laban. I bring with me my wives and children and many oxen, donkeys, sheep, goats and servants. I hope that I will find favor with you."

The messengers returned and said, "Your brother is coming to meet you with four hundred of his men."

Jacob was afraid. He remembered how he had tricked his brother and then fled from Canaan because of Esau's anger. Quickly, he divided his servants and flocks and camels into two groups thinking that if Esau destroyed one group, the other might escape. And he spoke to God and said, "O God of my fathers, I am doing as you have told me to do. I am returning to my own country. I am not worthy of your faithfulness. You have shown me great love, for I left Canaan with nothing but a staff of wood, and I return with so many people and animals that I can divide them into two companies. You have said that my descendants will number as the sand of the sea, and so I ask you to deliver me from the hand of my brother, Esau."

Jacob, with his people, stopped for the night and he set aside a gift of many goats, sheep, camels, cows and donkeys to give to Esau. He said to his servants, "Each of you take one of these herds and go on before me, leaving a space between the herds. When, in your turn, you meet my brother, tell him, 'These beasts are a gift for my lord Esau, a gift from his servant Jacob who follows behind.'" For Jacob hoped that this gift would soften his brother's heart, and that Esau would accept him when they met.

Before night fell, Jacob took his wives and children across the River Jabbok to a safer place. Then he returned alone to the camp to sleep.

But before he could lie down, a man was suddenly with him and began to wrestle with him. They wrestled all night until dawn began to break in the east, but neither one of them could best the other. When the other man saw that he could not win, he touched Jacob in the hollow of his hip, and Jacob's hip was put out of joint.

Then the man said, "Let me go, for dawn is breaking."

But Jacob said, "I will not let you go until you bless me."

And the other said to him, "What is your name?"

And he said, "Jacob."

Then the other said, "Your name shall no longer be Jacob, but Israel, for you have struggled with God and with humans and have overcome."

Jacob said, "But what is your name?"

The other said, "You do not need to ask my name." And he blessed him and was gone.

Then Jacob knew that he had seen God face to face.

The sun rose as he went to fetch his wives and children, limping because of his hip. As they came back across the river, he looked up and saw that Esau was coming. So he went in

front of his family, bowing to the ground seven times until he came near to his brother. But Esau ran to meet him and embraced him and they wept.

Esau said, "Who are all these people with you?"

"They are my wives and the children God has graciously given me," answered Jacob.

"And what about all the men and animals I met as I came along?"

"A gift," said Jacob, "for I hope that you will meet me in friendship."

"I have enough, my brother," said Esau. "Keep what you have for yourself."

"No," said Jacob. "I, too, have enough and I wish to give you this gift. Seeing your face when you greet me as a brother is like seeing the face of God." And so Esau accepted Jacob's gift.

Then Esau returned to his home. Jacob followed more slowly, because the children were not strong and the young animals could not be hurried. They came to Bethel, where Jacob had had the dream of the ladder to heaven so long ago. He stopped and built an altar because it was there that God had spoken to him.

They journeyed on, but before they came to Hebron where Isaac still lived, Rachel gave birth to a son. As he was being born, she gave him the name Benoni and then she died. But Jacob called him Benjamin.

Now Jacob had twelve sons: Reuben, the firstborn, and Simeon, Levi, Judah, Issachar, Zebulun, Dan, Naphtali, Gad, Asher, Joseph and Benjamin.

Jacob set a pillar upon Rachel's grave and then traveled until he came to his father, Isaac. Soon after, Isaac, who was old and full of days, breathed his last. His sons, Esau and Jacob, buried him.

Then Esau took his wives and children and all of his possessions and went into a land away from Canaan, for Canaan could not support the flocks of both Jacob and Esau. Esau's descendants populated and ruled over the hill country of Seir while Jacob and his sons settled in Canaan.

# JOSEPH AND HIS BROTHERS

Genesis 37.1-36. JACOB HAD TWELVE SONS. Ten of them were grown men who watched over their father's flocks and worked in the fields. Joseph, the eleventh-born, was still a boy and the youngest, Benjamin, was just a little child. They were all good sons, but Jacob loved Joseph the best.

Some people said that Joseph was the favorite because he was the first son of Jacob's most loved wife, Rachel, who had died when her second son, Benjamin, was born.

Others noticed that Jacob, who was growing old and spent his days sitting in the shade by his tent door, had time to talk with Joseph while the older sons, Reuben and Judah and the rest, worked. As Joseph grew he began to help his brothers with the grain harvest or the sheep shearing, but he would always go to Jacob afterward and tell him about what had happened during the day. Sometimes he spoke of one brother's carelessness or another's laziness. This made his brothers angry.

It angered them even more that Joseph was a dreamer. It seemed to them that he paid more attention to his dreams than to the dusty pastures and hungry flocks that they must look after.

"What do you dream that is so important?" they asked

him one day. "Why do you sit and pay no attention to the sheep or to us, your brothers?"

"I had a dream about you," Joseph answered. "I dreamed that we were all working in a field cutting wheat and bundling it into sheaves. Suddenly my sheaf, the one I had just bound up, rose and stood upright in the middle of the field. Your sheaves all turned toward mine and bowed low to it. I was just thinking about the meaning of this dream."

"It means that you think you are better than we are," said his brothers angrily, and they could not say a peaceable word to him.

Jacob saw that Joseph was growing tall. He was seventeen years old now, nearly a man, and Jacob thought it was time to give him a special gift. He had a coat made for Joseph. Not a short, sleeveless jacket such as his older brothers wore in the fields, but a fine coat woven of many colors of wool, a long coat with sleeves to the wrists.

As soon as the brothers saw it, they knew that the coat marked Joseph as their father's favorite son and they began to hate him.

"I had another dream," Joseph said one evening when all the brothers were gathered in their father's tent. "This one was wonderfully beautiful for the sun and the moon and the stars were all shining in the sky together. I saw the eleven brightest stars gather around the sun and the moon. Then they all – sun, moon and stars – bowed to me."

Even Jacob was displeased by this dream.

"How could it be that all of us, even your mother who is

dead, should bow to you?" he said. "Do not tell us such dreams." But when Jacob looked at Joseph's face, he knew that the boy was speaking truthfully. "Perhaps this vision has a meaning we do not yet know," he thought.

As for the brothers, they wished they never had to see Joseph again.

Perhaps that is why they took the flocks far from Hebron where Jacob dwelt, or perhaps they were only looking for better pastures as they told their father. When they had been gone for several days, Jacob said to Joseph, "Go to your brothers and the flocks at Shechem and see if all is well with them. Return soon and bring me news."

Joseph put on his fine coat since he was not going to work with his brothers but only to bring word of them to Jacob. It was a long walk, and when he came to Shechem, he was surprised to find that his brothers were not there. He wandered around the lonely land searching for them. At last he met a man who said, "I heard the sons of Jacob say that they were going on to Dothan."

So Joseph walked on to Dothan. He saw his brothers among the sheep and hurried a little, thinking of the food and water they would certainly offer him after his long journey.

The brothers saw him coming and were not pleased.

"Here comes the dreamer," one said. "Perhaps he has come to tell us another dream about how much better he is than the rest of us."

"The only way to stop his dreaming would be to kill him," said another, half joking.

"That would not be hard to do," said yet another. "And no

one would ever know. We could throw his body into one of the dry pits below the hill and say that he was devoured by wild animals."

Once the words had been spoken, the brothers all began thinking about this plan. But Reuben, the oldest, said, "No. We cannot have our brother's blood on our hands. Throw him into one of the pits. No one will find him and we will not have shed his blood." He looked at his brothers' faces. They were stiff with hatred but one after another they agreed.

By now Joseph was near. His brothers rose up. Instead of greeting him, they seized him. They tore off the coat that had been a gift from their father and threw him into one of the pits.

The pit had been dug to collect water, but it was dry now and deep. Joseph was bruised and stunned. He could see nothing but the dark walls of the pit and a circle of blue sky.

Reuben went away from the others to another pasture. "I will return in the night," he thought. "Then I can pull Joseph from the pit and take him to our father."

The others got food from their packs. As they sat down to eat, they looked across the valley and saw a caravan of Ishmaelites coming from Gilead. They were journeying toward Egypt with sweet-smelling resins and balm to sell.

"Look," said Judah. "Those traders will buy anything. Why not sell Joseph as a slave? If we leave him in the pit, he will die, and we will be guilty of his death just as if we had killed him outright. If we sell him, we will profit by it, and Joseph and his dreams will be gone from us forever."

And so it was done. The nine brothers pulled Joseph from

the pit and sold him for twenty pieces of silver, which they divided among themselves. And Joseph was tied by his bound wrists to one of the camels and led away toward Egypt.

When night fell, Reuben came to the pit and found it empty. He rushed to his brothers and said, "What have you done with Joseph?"

"We have sold him," they said. "He has gone to Egypt where he will live a fine life as a slave."

"And our father?" asked Reuben. "What will we tell our father?"

"Don't worry," they said. "We will kill a goat and dip that special coat of Joseph's in its blood. We will have a story for our father."

And so the ten brothers returned to Jacob and gave him the blood-soaked coat. "We found this," they said. "Could it be your son's?"

Jacob knew it at once. "It is Joseph's!" he cried. "He has been killed by wild animals. He has surely been torn to pieces and I will not see him again in this life."

And Jacob ripped his clothes and mourned for days and months. None of his sons could comfort him.

But Joseph was not dead. He was a slave in Egypt.

# JOSEPH IN EGYPT

Genesis 41.1-45.28,
47.27-28, 49.1-28.

PHARAOH, THE MIGHTY RULER of Egypt, had a dream one night which troubled him so deeply that he sent for all the magicians and wise men of his realm. He told them what he had dreamed. Then he said, "What is the meaning of this dream? You must tell me."

But none of them could. They consulted their oracles and their scrolls but they could only shake their heads.

"Who will help me?' said Pharaoh. "I cannot forget my dream."

The servant who carried Pharaoh's golden cup bowed before him and spoke.

"O Most High," he said, "there is a man called Joseph, a slave from the land of Canaan. I came to know him two years ago when I was imprisoned because I had displeased you. He is a prisoner and a slave, but even the governor of the prison trusts him and gives him great responsibility. I told Joseph a dream I had, and he told me that it meant I would be restored to my office and be cupbearer to Pharaoh once more. What he said was true. Send for him, Most High, that he might serve you."

So messengers came to Joseph in prison. They gave him water to wash himself and new clothes to put on. Then they brought him before Pharaoh.

Pharaoh looked at him. "I am told that you are gifted at interpreting dreams," he said.

Joseph answered, "Since I was a boy, God has given me an understanding of dreams. It is God who will tell me the meaning of Pharaoh's dream."

"Listen," said Pharaoh. "It seemed that I stood on the bank of the Nile, the river that gives life to Egypt, and I saw seven sleek and fat cows come out of the river to graze. Then came seven more cows but they were ugly and thin. They ate up the seven sleek and fat cows, yet they remained as thin and ugly as before. Then I had another dream. Seven ears of grain, plump and good, were growing on one stalk. Then seven thin and blighted ears grew on the same stalk and swallowed up the seven full ears. These dreams trouble me, yet my wisest men cannot tell me what they mean."

"The two dreams are one dream," said Joseph, "and in them God has revealed to Pharaoh what will surely come to be. The seven fat cows and the seven good ears are seven years of fine weather and abundant crops. The seven lean cows and the seven empty ears are seven years of drought and bad harvests. This is what God will bring to Egypt. Seven years of great plenty will be followed by seven years of famine. Unless some of the plenty is stored up to be used in the bad years, the famine will consume the land of Egypt. This is what God has shown you. You must choose a man of good judgment who will see that God's warning is heeded and Egypt will be saved."

"You are that man," said Pharaoh. And he gave Joseph a ring from his own finger and a gold chain to wear around his neck.

And so Joseph, who had been sold into slavery by his jealous brothers, became second only to Pharaoh in all Egypt.

Everything came to pass as Pharaoh's dream foretold. During the seven good years, Joseph, now appointed viceroy of all Egypt, traveled the length and breadth of the land seeing that great storehouses were built for the rich harvests. When the years of famine came, people needing grain were required to come to Joseph with their requests.

The famine was widespread and people in many lands beyond Egypt suffered from hunger, but only in Egypt had grain been stored up. So all the world came to Joseph to buy grain.

In Canaan, Joseph's own family was running out of food. His father, Jacob, heard that there was grain in Egypt, so he sent his ten older sons to buy what they could to keep the family from starvation. He did not send Benjamin, his youngest son, for he believed that Joseph whom he had loved so greatly was dead, and he did not want to lose Benjamin, too.

Of course, like everyone else, the sons of Jacob had to come before the viceroy of all Egypt to buy the grain. As they journeyed across the dry land they thought of the brother they had sold into slavery long ago, but they did not know him when they bowed before him.

How could they?

Joseph was now a tall, imposing man with the gold chain of his office around his neck. He wore the headdress and robes of a high official and was called by an Egyptian name. But he knew them at once. They were his brothers. But where was Benjamin?

As they bowed down before him, he remembered the dream he had had when he was only a boy, of their sheaves of grain bowing down to his.

"Who are you and where do you come from?" he asked in a harsh voice.

"We are from the land of Canaan," they said. "We come to buy food." They spoke in Hebrew and, hearing it, Joseph almost wept. But he waited for the interpreter to translate their answer into Egyptian.

Then he said, "I think you are spies."

The brothers were afraid. What if this grand Egyptian threw them into prison?

"No," they said. "We are brothers, the sons of one man. We have come to buy grain."

"Has your father sent all his sons?" asked Joseph.

"There were twelve of us. One was lost long ago, and our father still misses him so much that he would not let his youngest son come with us. He keeps him close to him always."

"I am not sure I can believe this story," said Joseph. "But I will sell you grain on the condition that one of you stays here, in prison, until you return with your youngest brother. Then I will believe you."

The brothers looked at one another. "Surely God is punishing us for selling Joseph into slavery," they thought. But they agreed to leave Simeon in Egypt. Then they took their grain and returned to their father.

When Jacob heard what they had done, he lamented greatly and at first refused to let them take Benjamin to Egypt.

"I have lost Joseph," he said, "and now Simeon. If Benjamin goes to Egypt he will never return."

But in time the grain ran out. They were again threatened with starvation and Jacob could do nothing but allow his sons to set out for Egypt once more, taking Benjamin with them.

When Joseph heard that his brothers had arrived, he ordered his servants to prepare a feast and bring all of them, including Simeon, to his house. They came before him and bowed. Then they gave him gifts, saying, "Our father has sent you sweet-smelling gum and resin and honey and almonds."

"So the old man, your father, lives?" said Joseph.

"He lives," said the brothers.

Then Joseph looked at the face of Benjamin, the other son of his mother, Rachel. In the years he had been in Egypt this little brother had grown to be a man. Suddenly he was overcome with love for his brothers and hurried into another room and wept. When he returned, he amazed them all by seating them at the table in the order of their birth. Then they feasted together and were merry.

Afterward, while his brothers slept, Joseph had their donkeys loaded with grain. But in the sack upon Benjamin's donkey, he placed his own great silver cup.

In the morning the brothers departed, thinking that now they could all return to their father, but they were soon overtaken by Joseph's steward.

"Why have you returned evil for good?" he demanded of them. "You have stolen the great silver cup from which my master drinks."

They protested that they had not stolen anything. "If you

find the cup," said Reuben, "you can do what you want with the man who has it."

At once the steward opened the sack upon Benjamin's donkey and drew out the cup. They were all horrified. They had promised their father faithfully that Benjamin would return to him unharmed. And so they all went back to the city with the steward.

When they were brought before Joseph they bowed to the ground. Judah spoke, "O Great Viceroy of Egypt, hear me. We do not know how the cup came to be in our brother's sack. But since it was there, allow me to remain with you in slavery. Our father had two sons by his beloved wife, Rachel. One of them was lost to him long years ago. Only Benjamin remains. If Benjamin does not return to Canaan with us, our father will surely die."

Joseph could no longer hide the truth. He sent all of the Egyptians out of the room and said, "My brothers, don't you know me? I am Joseph, the brother you sold into Egypt. But do not be distressed, for you carried out the purpose of God. There have been two years of famine. There will be five more. But because God put a dream into Pharaoh's mind and gave me the gift of telling its meaning, there is food enough in Egypt for all. Now go to my father and tell him that his son Joseph lives, and that God has made him ruler over the land of Egypt. Then gather up all your households and come to me. I will give you land in Goshen. And so your people will prosper."

Then he embraced Benjamin and wept and all the brothers embraced. When they had talked about everything that

had happened in the years that Joseph had been in Egypt, the eleven brothers went again to Canaan with messages and gifts from Joseph and Pharaoh.

When they told Jacob that Joseph was alive and ruler over Egypt, he could not believe them. But they told him the whole story and showed him the wagons and supplies that Joseph had sent to help them on their long journey.

Then Jacob said, "Enough! I must go and see my son before I die."

So the sons of Jacob gathered up all their children and wives and came again to Egypt with their father and settled in the land of Goshen.

Jacob lived in Egypt for seventeen years. Before he died, he blessed each of his twelve sons, and their descendants were afterward known as the twelve tribes of Israel.

And in Egypt the people of Israel flourished for many generations.

# JOCHEBED AND MIRIAM
## SAVE MOSES

HE DESCENDANTS of the twelve sons of Jacob lived in Egypt for many years after the time of Joseph. They were the keepers of Pharaoh's herds and they prospered and multiplied.

Exodus 1.6-2.10.

But after ten generations, a pharaoh came to power who knew nothing of Joseph and how he had served Egypt. He did not believe that the children of Israel were useful workers to be respected. He saw that the whole region of Goshen was filled with Israelites and that in all of Egypt they outnumbered the Egyptians.

Pharaoh became afraid. The Israelites, he thought, might turn against Egypt in time of war. "There are more of them every year," he said to himself, "and they are too independent and strong. I will make them slaves and set them to do hard labor. Then they will become a weak people and will not be a danger to Egypt."

He appointed overseers who forced the Israelites to dig canals and build dams, to cut great blocks of stone and drag them to the places where new cities were being built, and most especially, to make endless thousands of bricks out of mud and straw.

In spite of hard labor and cruel treatment the Israelites still grew in number. Pharaoh called before him two Hebrew women, Shiphrah and Puah. They were midwives who attended women when their babies were being born. He said to them, "When you see that one of the Israelite babies is a boy, you must kill the child."

But Shiphrah and Puah knew that it would be wrong before God to do this, and they made sure that all the babies lived.

Pharaoh called them again and said, "Why have you not obeyed me?"

They answered, "The Hebrew women are strong. The babies are born before we can get there. We are not able to do as you command."

So Pharaoh ordered all of his people to search out baby boys born to Israelite families and throw them in the Nile River.

The land of Goshen was filled with sorrow and weeping. The power of Pharaoh was absolute, and it seemed that the people were helpless.

But there was a very determined woman of the tribe of Levi who refused to believe that nothing could be done. Her name was Jochebed. She had a daughter called Miriam, who was eleven years old, and a little son called Aaron. Now she was expecting another child. As she waited for her baby to be born, she struggled to think of a way to save him — if he was a boy.

And he was a boy, healthy and vigorous and beautiful as all babies are beautiful. While he was tiny Jochebed kept him hidden in their little dark house near the river. Miriam helped, holding her baby brother, entertaining him with games and soothing him with songs.

But the baby grew. He was three months old. Already he was not always content to be quiet. His body and voice were strong. He would be found.

Jochebed made a plan. She knew the river well — all the plants that grew there and the people who came there.

"I will make a little boat," she said to Miriam. "We will set the baby afloat on the water. He will be on the river, not in it."

"But what will happen to him?" asked Miriam. "He can't live on the water."

"You will see what happens," said her mother. "You will be watching from the shore."

Jochebed gathered strong papyrus leaves that grew in the shallow water of the river and wove a basket that was shaped like a little boat. She wove it tight and made a lid for it with a hinge. Then she covered the outside of the basket with pitch to make it waterproof and left it to dry overnight.

When dawn came she nursed the baby, wrapped him well and lulled him to sleep. Then she gently placed him in the basket-boat and closed the lid so that he would be protected from the sun.

She called Miriam. "Come," she said, "for today you must do the most important job you will ever do."

Together they went to the quiet water at the edge of the river and set the little boat afloat among the bulrushes that grew there.

"He will not drift far," said Jochebed, "for the rushes will catch the basket. And I think someone will find it here."

"Who will find it?" said Miriam. "What will they do with my brother?"

"Wait and watch. You will know what to do," said her mother, and she went home.

Miriam stayed as close to the basket as she dared. Through the rushes she could see fishermen and washerwomen coming to the river, but they were intent upon their work and did not notice the basket floating so quietly.

The sun rose higher. Miriam saw that the washerwomen and fishermen were hurrying away and soon she knew why. Pharaoh's daughter had come to the river to bathe. Miriam stayed perfectly still as the princess sent away all her servants except her own maid. Just as the princess was ready to step into the water, she turned her head as if she heard a sound.

Miriam heard it, too.

"The baby is whimpering," she thought in despair. "He is hungry." She almost went to him but she remembered her mother's words, "Wait and watch." So she did not move.

The princess peered through the reeds. "What is that floating in the water?" she asked her maidservant. "Go and bring it to me."

When the basket was before the princess, she lifted the lid and saw the baby. He cried harder for a moment, startled by the light, and then stopped and gazed up at her solemnly. Pharaoh's daughter looked long at the little face with its bright eyes.

"He is one of the children of Israel," she said softly. "How beautiful he is. Well, no one shall harm him. No one."

Miriam had crept close. When she heard these words her

heart was filled with joy. But still she wondered, what would the princess do with her small brother?

"I will call him Moses, for I have plucked him from the water," the princess went on. "He will be brought up in my palace."

"He will need a woman to nurse him," said the maid. "He is very young."

"I will find one," said the princess, and she looked up and down the river as if she expected a woman to appear.

Suddenly Miriam knew what her important job was. Shyly she stepped from among the reeds. She forgot to bow her head to the princess.

"I know a woman," she said. "She could nurse the baby."

"Bring her here," said Pharaoh's daughter.

Miriam ran home. Jochebed was sitting just inside the door of the little house waiting, it seemed, for Miriam. Miriam could hardly say a word, she had run so fast, but her mother saw her face and rose.

"Take me to her," she said.

The princess was holding the baby when Jochebed and Miriam came to the river. She looked long into their faces. Then she spoke, "This child is named Moses," she said. "I ask that you take him and keep him as long as he needs to be nursed. Then he will come to my palace and he will be my son."

And so it was that Moses was saved by the wit of his mother, the care of his sister and the kindness of Pharaoh's daughter.

# MOSES ANSWERS THE CALL
# OF GOD

MOSES LIVED with his own mother and his sister, Miriam, and his brother, Aaron, in their little house in the Hebrew village until he was no longer a baby but a little boy. Then his mother brought him to Pharaoh's daughter and said, "I have cared for this child with great joy. But now he is old enough to live with you as we agreed when you found him in the river."

Exodus 2.11- 4.20.

And so Moses grew up in the palaces of Egypt as the son of Pharaoh's daughter. He grew tall and strong and wore the linen clothing and gold chains that were fitting for an Egyptian prince. But he did not forget that he was not an Egyptian. He remembered the Hebrew village and his family. He remembered that the children of Israel were his people.

Moses often went out to see the building of the great monuments that Pharaoh had ordered for his glory. And he watched the Hebrew slaves making bricks of mud and straw and carrying heavy loads.

One day he saw an Egyptian overseer beating a Hebrew laborer. Instead of passing by, he looked at the Hebrew's face and thought, "This is one of my people. I can watch no longer." Moses looked all around him. There was no one nearby, so he shouted at the Hebrew man to run. Then he killed the Egyptian and hid his body in the sand.

The next day he went out again and this time he saw two Hebrews fighting. He could see that one was in the wrong and he said to him, "Why do you strike your fellow Hebrew?"

The man looked at him angrily and said, "Who made you a prince and a judge over me? Are you going to kill me as you killed the Egyptian?"

Then Moses realized that the thing he had done was known and talked about, and he was afraid. And indeed, Pharaoh himself heard of it and sent out orders that Moses should be caught and killed.

So Moses fled far away to the land of Midian, a dry desert country, very different from the fertile land of Egypt. One day he sat down by a well and there he met the seven daughters of Jethro, a priest of the Midianites. They had come to draw water for their flock of sheep. But just as they filled the troughs so that the sheep could drink, some shepherds came and said, "This water is just what we need for our sheep." And they started to drive the young women away.

When Moses saw what the shepherds intended to do, he stepped forward and said, "This water is not for you." The shepherds, seeing his strength and firmness, went away and Jethro's daughters watered their sheep.

Afterward they told their father what had happened and he said, "Invite the man to break bread with us. Don't leave him alone in the desert." And Moses came to live near Jethro, and in time he married Zipporah, one of his daughters.

During the many years that Moses lived in the land of

Midian, the pharaoh of Egypt died and a new pharaoh reigned. But the Hebrews' lives did not get better. They groaned under their slavery and cried out to God to help them. And God remembered his covenant with Abraham, with Isaac and with Jacob. And he remembered Moses.

One day Moses was keeping Jethro's flock and he took it as far as Mount Sinai, which was also called the mountain of God. Suddenly he saw that a bush growing on the mountainside was on fire. The fire was at the heart of the bush and it blazed brightly, but the bush did not burn up. Moses gazed and could not understand. Then he heard a voice call, "Moses! Moses!"

"Here I am," he answered.

Then the voice said, "Come no closer, but remove your sandals, for you stand in a holy place. I am the God of Abraham and Isaac and of all your ancestors. I have seen the misery of my people who are in Egypt. Now I will see that they leave this land of suffering and go to a good and broad land, a land flowing with milk and honey, the land of Canaan. Go to Pharaoh. Tell him he must let my people go. Then you may lead them out of Egypt."

Moses was amazed. "Who am I to do this thing?" he asked. "And what shall I say to the people?"

"Assemble all the elders of Israel. Tell them that the God of their fathers, of Abraham, Isaac and Jacob, has heard their cries, and that he has sent you to lead them out of Egypt to the Promised Land. Then go to Pharaoh and ask him to let the Hebrews go on a three-day journey into the wilderness to make a sacrifice to the Lord their God. He will not let you go

at first. But I will strike the Egyptians with wonders I shall perform, and then he will let you go."

Moses said, "But what if no one believes me? What if they say that God has never spoken to me?"

God asked him, "What do you hold in your hand?"

Moses answered, "My staff."

"Throw it on the ground," said God.

Moses threw his staff on the ground and it became a snake. He turned to run away but God said, "Put out your hand. Catch it by the tail."

And when Moses did as God said, the snake became a staff again.

"Now," said the Lord. "Put your hand inside your coat."

Moses did and when he took it out again his hand was white with leprous sores.

"Put it in again," said God. And Moses did and when he drew it out, it was healthy!

God said, "These are signs I am giving to you so that the people will know that you have truly seen God. If they do not believe the first sign or the second sign and will not listen, take water from the Nile and spill it on dry ground. It will turn to blood."

But Moses was still afraid. "I do not speak well," he said. "My tongue is slow and I have no gift with words."

"I will give you the words," said God.

But still Moses said, "O my Lord, please send someone else!"

Then God spoke with anger. "Do you think you are alone? Even now your brother, Aaron, is coming out to meet you. He speaks well and he will speak when you cannot. Do not argue any longer. Return to Egypt."

And so Moses, with Zipporah and their sons, returned to Egypt to do God's bidding.

# MOSES AND THE PLAGUES
# OF EGYPT

Exodus 4.27-10.28. MOSES AND AARON met near the mountain of God and greeted each other with affection. Moses told his brother everything the Lord had said to him, and he showed him the signs and wonders he had been commanded to perform. They called together the elders of the Hebrew people. Aaron spoke the words that God had spoken to Moses, and Moses showed them the signs and wonders. Then the children of Israel knew that God remembered them, and they bowed their heads and worshiped.

Now Moses and Aaron went to Pharaoh and said, "The God of Israel says, 'Let my people go into the wilderness and hold a feast to honor me.' Give us leave to go on a three-day journey into the desert so that we may worship him in this way."

Pharaoh said, "No. I know nothing of this God and I will not let the people of Israel go. You, Moses and Aaron, you only want to take these people away from their work. You have duties yourselves. Go back to them."

When they had left, Pharaoh summoned his overseers and said, "The Israelites are lazy. They wish to escape from their work. From this day on, I order you to give them no straw to mix with the mud when they are making bricks. Instead they must collect their own straw. And tell them that they must make the same number of bricks as they did yesterday. We will make sure that they have no time to listen to lies and think of going into the wilderness to worship their God."

The slave drivers carried out Pharaoh's orders and beat the Hebrew foremen when they saw that fewer bricks were being made.

And the people said to Moses, "May the Lord punish you. We have to wander the land in search of straw, we are beaten and our lives are harder than ever. You have brought the hatred of Pharaoh upon us."

Then Moses went again to the Lord and said, "Why did you send me back? I have done what you told me to do, but the people of Israel are driven harder than ever. You have not saved them."

The Lord said, "Now you will see how my mighty hand shall force Pharaoh to let my people go. I know how my people suffer and I shall free them from their bondage. Egypt will know that I am the Lord. All of my promises will be fulfilled."

But when Moses told the people what the Lord had said, they did not believe him. Their hearts were too heavy and the burden of their slavery was too great.

The Lord said, "Go again to Pharaoh and tell him to let my people go."

"If my own people will not listen to me, why should Pharaoh hear my words? When I speak my tongue stumbles," said Moses.

"Look," said the Lord. "Say to your brother, Aaron, everything that I have said to you. He will be your prophet and speak the words to Pharaoh. And show Pharaoh the signs and wonders I have given to you. Do this, although he will not listen until I have performed greater wonders."

Moses and Aaron did as God said. They went to Pharaoh. Aaron spoke and threw down his staff and it became a snake. Pharaoh immediately called for his sorcerers and each of them threw down a staff and they all became snakes. But Aaron's staff swallowed up all of the others. And, as the Lord had said, Pharaoh hardened his heart and did not listen. He would not let the people of Israel go.

And then the Lord sent plagues to Egypt.

First he sent the plague of blood. He said to Moses, "Tell Aaron to strike the water of the river with his staff, and all of the rivers and streams and ditches and ponds in Egypt will turn to blood."

Moses and Aaron did as the Lord said and all the water turned to blood. The fish died and people had to dig in the ground for water to drink. The plague lasted for seven days but Pharaoh would not be moved.

When the seven days had passed, the Lord said to Moses, "Tell Pharaoh that unless he lets my people go, I will send a plague of frogs over the land."

Again Pharaoh hardened his heart.

Aaron stretched his staff over the river and from all the waters of Egypt came frogs. They entered every house, even Pharaoh's palace. They climbed into the cooking pans and the wash basins and onto the beds.

Pharaoh said, "Tomorrow ask the Lord to take the frogs away and I will let your people go."

And the Lord made all the frogs die and the people piled them in great piles and they stank. But Pharaoh saw that the frogs were gone from his palace and so he would not keep his promise to Moses and Aaron.

Then the Lord told Moses to tell Aaron to stretch forth his staff and strike the dust of the land. And the dust was turned to gnats on people and beasts all over Egypt.

But still Pharaoh's heart was hardened and he would not listen to Moses.

The Lord said to Moses, "Wait for Pharaoh as he goes to the river. Say that if he does not let my people go to worship me in the wilderness, I will send a plague of flies. His palace and the houses of all his people will be filled with swarms of flies. But the land of Goshen, where my people live, will have no flies. And this will happen tomorrow."

Pharaoh did not listen to Moses and the next day Egypt was infested with flies. Pharaoh sent for Moses and Aaron and said, "All right. You may make a sacrifice to your God, but you must do it here."

Moses said, "Your people here will not understand the way we worship. They will throw stones at us. We must travel for three days into the wilderness."

"I will let you go," said Pharaoh. "But do not go far and pray for me."

"I will ask God to remove the plague," said Moses. And the Lord took every fly away, but Pharaoh forgot his promise and did not let the people go.

Then the Lord said to Moses, "Now tell Pharaoh that I will bring a plague upon the horses and donkeys and cattle and sheep and goats of the Egyptians, and they will die. And this will happen tomorrow. But nothing that belongs to the children of Israel will die."

Again Pharaoh did not listen to Moses and the next day he sent his men out to see what had happened. And indeed, the animals of his people had died. But still he did not let the Hebrew people go.

The Lord said to Moses, "Fill your hands with soot from the ovens and go before Pharaoh and throw it into the air. Egypt will be filled with fine dust that will make boils erupt on people throughout the land."

And so it happened, but Pharaoh's heart remained hard toward the people of Israel.

Now the Lord said to Moses, "Say to Pharaoh that I will send more plagues upon him and his people so that he will know my power. He does not understand that I could stretch out my hand and destroy him and all his people. He uses his power against my people and will not let them go. Well, his power is nothing to mine. Tomorrow I will send a hailstorm greater than any that has been seen since the beginning of Egypt. He should tell his people to bring in their herds, for the hail will kill every man and every animal that is not under shelter."

Moses said all of these things to Pharaoh, but Pharaoh said nothing to his people. Yet some, who heard Moses' words and feared the power of the Lord, ran to bring in their servants and cattle.

And as the Lord had directed, Moses lifted his staff and a great storm with thunder and lightning came down from

heaven. The hailstones were so heavy that they knocked down everything left out in all the fields of Egypt – people, animals and even trees fell to the ground. But in Goshen, where the Hebrews lived, there was no hail.

Pharaoh sent for Moses and Aaron and said, "This time I have sinned. Your Lord is right and I am wrong. Ask him to stop the storm and the hail and I will let your people go."

Moses said, "I will go out of the city and raise my hand to the Lord and there will be no more hail. You say that you have sinned, but I know that you still will not let the people go."

And all that Moses said happened. The storm stopped but Pharaoh did not let the people go.

Moses and Aaron went before Pharaoh and said, "The Lord our God says, 'How long will you refuse to bow before me? When will you let my people go so that they can worship me? If you do not let them go, I will send a plague of locusts which will cover your land and eat every plant and leaf and blade of grass that is still standing after the storm. No plague like it has been seen by your fathers and the fathers of your fathers.'" And Moses and Aaron left the palace.

Now some of Pharaoh's men said, "Let these people go and worship their God, before Egypt is destroyed."

So Pharaoh called Moses back and said, "Go and worship the Lord your God. But first tell me how many of you will go?"

Moses said, "We will all go, our old and our young, our sons and our daughters, and we will take all our flocks and herds so that we can have a feast to honor the Lord."

But Pharaoh said, "Do you think I will let you take your children? You are deceiving me. The men alone may go to worship. Isn't that what you have been asking for?" And he threw Moses out of the palace.

Then Moses did as the Lord told him to and stretched his staff out over Egypt and an east wind began to blow. It blew all day and all night and it brought in locusts. They covered the face of the earth and ate until no green leaf or fruit remained.

Then Pharaoh sent for Moses and Aaron to come quickly. He said, "I have sinned. I beg you, ask your God to take this death away from me and my land."

And Moses prayed and the Lord turned the wind to blow from the west, and it blew all the locusts away into the Red Sea. Not one remained. And when they were gone, Pharaoh said, "No, I will not let the people of Israel go."

Now the Lord told Moses to stretch his hand to heaven and a thick darkness covered Egypt. The people could not move from one place to another, for they could not see at all. But in the houses of the Hebrews there was light.

Pharaoh sent for Moses and said, "All right. You may go and take your families with you, but leave your flocks and herds behind."

Moses said, "Our animals must go with us so that we can make offerings at our feast."

Then Pharaoh changed his mind. "I will not let your people go," he said. "And I order you never to come before me again. If I see your face, you will die."

Moses answered, "You will never see my face again."

But the Lord knew that he was not finished with Pharaoh and neither was Moses.

# ESCAPE FROM EGYPT

Exodus 11.1-12.34,
13.17-15.21. GOD SAID TO MOSES, "I will bring one more plague upon Pharaoh and his land. It will be so terrible that he will beg the Israelites to leave Egypt." And he told Moses what he was going to do.

Moses went to Pharaoh and said, "I came because you can save your people from terrible suffering. The Lord has told me that he will now send the greatest plague of all. At midnight on a certain day, every firstborn in the land of Egypt will die. The firstborn of Pharaoh will die. So will the firstborn of the maidservant grinding wheat and every firstborn animal. There will be such grief and wailing in Egypt as has never been before or ever will be again. But no harm will come to the Israelites. Then your officials will bow to us and ask us to go."

In spite of this warning, Pharaoh still refused to let the people of Israel go out of his land.

Then God spoke again to Moses. He told him what the Israelites must do so that they would be spared this most terrible of plagues.

Moses called the elders of his people and said, "No harm will come to the children of Israel if we heed the words of the Lord. On the fourteenth day of this month, the congregation of Israel will come together and slaughter a lamb for each

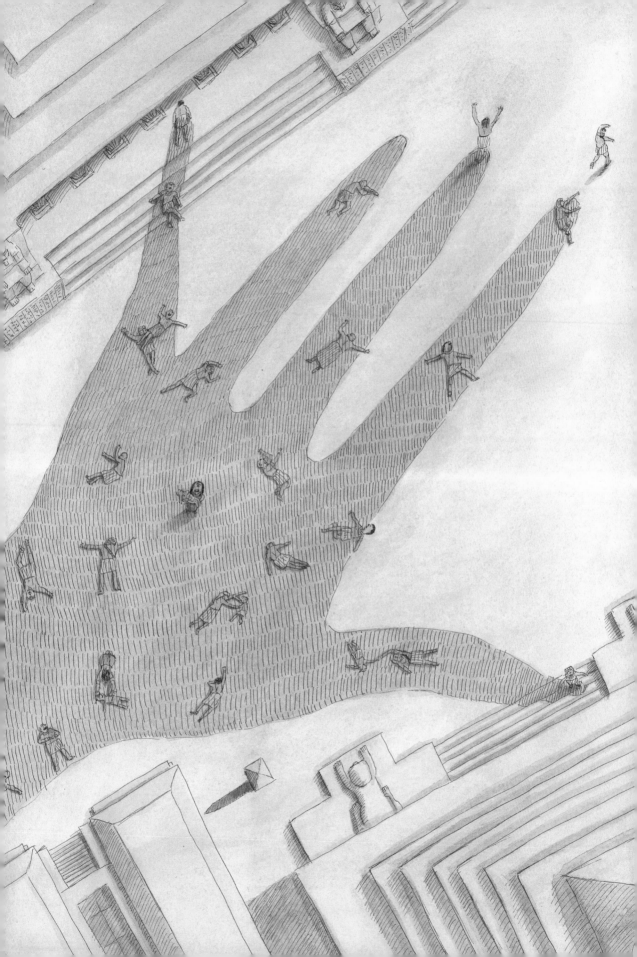

household. We will take some of the blood and paint it on the doorposts and above the door of each house. Then we will roast the meat and eat it with unleavened bread and bitter herbs, with our coats and shoes on and our staffs in our hands. For this is the night when the Lord will move through Egypt and strike down every firstborn. The blood on the doorways will be a sign that the children of Israel are inside. The Lord will see the blood and pass over and our firstborns shall not die. The Lord commands that we remember this day of Passover, and that we teach our children and our children's children to remember it forever."

All happened as the Lord told Moses it would. While the Hebrews did exactly as they had been commanded and sat safely together in their houses, every firstborn in every Egyptian household was struck down. Pharaoh rose in the night and so did all his court and all of Egypt, and there was wailing in every house.

Now Pharaoh called Moses and Aaron to him. He said, "Get out of Egypt, you and all the Israelites, and take all your children and all your flocks with you, as you have wanted to." And the Egyptians hurried the Hebrews, saying, "Go quickly! If you do not leave our land, we will all die."

So the people had to leave in the clothes they were wearing, carrying pots of unleavened dough wrapped in their cloaks, for they had prepared no provisions. There were about six hundred thousand men on foot with their families and all their flocks and herds of cattle. And that day was four hundred and thirty years to the day since the Israelites had come into the land of Egypt.

The Lord went before the people in a pillar of cloud by day

and a pillar of fire by night so that they could travel without stopping and would not lose their way. And he led them through the wilderness to the marshes beside the Red Sea, and there they made camp.

Now Pharaoh realized that the people of Israel had truly fled from him. They were gone. He and his courtiers began to think about the great amount of work the Israelites had done for them. Who would do it now? And so Pharaoh changed his mind. He ordered up his own chariot and all the chariots of Egypt and all the best warriors and set out in pursuit of the fleeing people.

The Israelites saw the Egyptians coming and they were afraid. They cried out to Moses, "Why did you bring us here to die in the wilderness? Didn't we tell you to leave us alone? It would better to be in Egypt serving the Egyptians than to die here!"

The Lord said to Moses, "There is no reason for the people to cry out against you and against me. Tell them to go forward. Stretch your hand out over the waters of the sea and they will be able to cross it on dry ground."

And the pillar of cloud went and stood between the Israelites and the army of Egypt. The pillar of fire lit up the night and the Egyptian army could come no closer.

Then Moses stretched his hand out over the sea. And God sent a strong east wind that blew all night and divided the water and made a path of dry land through the middle of the sea. The children of Israel began to hurry along that path with a wall of water rising up beside them on their right and on their left.

The Egyptians came swiftly after them, warriors and horses and chariots. As morning came, the Lord saw how close the Egyptians were to the people and he caused the wheels of the chariots to lock so that they could not move. Then the Egyptians said, "Truly their God is protecting them," and they tried to turn back.

The Israelites rushed on and reached the far shore of the sea.

Then the Lord said to Moses, "Stretch your hand once again over the sea."

Moses stretched out his hand, and as day broke the water poured back to where it had always been. It swept over the Egyptians. Not one of them escaped.

Moses and the Israelites looked back and saw how the Lord had defeated the Egyptians and they sang a song of praise:

> I will sing a song to the Lord,
> He has triumphed with glory,
> He has thrown horse and rider into the sea.
> The Lord is my strength and my song,
> And he has become my salvation,
> He is my God, and I will praise him.

Then Miriam, sister of Moses and Aaron, took a tambourine in her hand and led the women in dance and they sang:

> Yes, sing to the Lord,
> He has triumphed with glory,
> He has thrown horse and rider into the sea.
> He is my God, and I will praise him.

So Moses brought the children of Israel out of Egypt.

# IN THE WILDERNESS

Exodus 15.22-
16.31, 19.1-20.21,
24.12-18, 32.1-20,
34.1-35.35, 39.1-43;
Numbers 6.22-27,
14.1-31, 20.2-13;
Deuteronomy
31.14-23, 32.48-52,
34.1-12.

Now the Israelites were free from slavery in Egypt, but they had come to a barren wilderness of dry earth and forbidding mountains, not the land of milk and honey they had been promised. For three days they found no water, and when at last they came to a place called Marah where there was a spring, the water was bitter and they could not drink it.

The people complained, "What are we going to drink?"

Moses cried out to the Lord and the Lord showed him a piece of wood. "Cast it into the water," he said.

Moses did this and the water became sweet.

The people drank deeply and drew water for their animals. Then they went on, but the way was difficult and nothing grew in the land. A month passed and another was halfway gone when the people began to complain to Moses again.

"We could have stayed in Egypt and died there with bread in our mouths. Have you brought us here to starve together?"

Moses and Aaron spoke to the people. "The Lord hears your grumbling," they said. "You say you are complaining against us, but truly you are grumbling against the Lord. And now he has told us that he will give you flesh to eat in the evening and bread in the morning."

The people waited to see what this might mean. In the evening, flock after flock of quails came to the place where they were camped. They were able to snare enough birds to cook a good meal. Still they were not convinced that the Lord could give them bread in the wilderness.

But in the morning the ground was covered with small white flakes such as none of them had ever seen before.

"It is the bread that the Lord has promised us," said Moses.

So the people started to gather up the flakes though they still did not believe it was bread. When they put it in their mouths, they were surprised to find that it tasted like wafers made with honey and was pleasant to eat.

Moses saw that they liked this bread and he said, "It is called manna. Gather only as much as you need today, for tomorrow the Lord will give it to us again."

Some of the people did not believe what Moses said and gathered extra manna to keep for the next day. In the morning it was full of worms and it stank. Moses was angry.

"When will you listen to me?" he asked. "The Lord has kept his word today and so he will every day."

And it was true. In all their years of wandering, until they came to the borders of Canaan, the children of Israel ate manna.

In the third month of their wandering they came to Mount Sinai, where the Lord had spoken to Moses from the burning bush. They made camp there, at the foot of the mountain.

Now God called to Moses from the mountain and said, "Say this to the house of Israel. You have seen what I did to the Egyptians, and how I have brought you here where I will speak to you. If you listen to my voice and keep faith with me, you will be my particular treasure and a holy nation."

When Moses told the people what God had said, they spoke as one, "We will do all that the Lord has asked."

Moses carried the people's answer to God, and God said, "I will speak to you from a cloud and all the people will hear me and they will believe you forever. Tell them to purify themselves and wash their clothing and I will come down on Mount Sinai on the third day."

In the morning of the third day, a great storm descended upon the mountain with thunder and lightning. Then a tremendous trumpet blast made the people tremble, but they gathered at the foot of the mountain. It was wrapped in smoke because the Lord had come in fire. The mountain shook and the trumpet sounded louder and louder. Moses spoke to God and God answered him in thunder.

The people moved back from the smoke and the thunder and they said to Moses, "You speak to God. We will believe you and do as you say. Only do not let God speak to us or we will die."

So Moses went alone up into the darkness. The Lord gave him commandments to take to the children of Israel:

I am the Lord your God. Have no other gods before me.
Do not make idols or images and bow down to them and
serve them.
Do not speak the name of the Lord thy God except to
worship and honor him.
Remember that the seventh day is the Sabbath and keep
it holy.

Honor your father and your mother.

Do not murder.

Do not commit adultery.

Do not steal.

Do not say untrue things about your neighbor.

Do not covet anything that belongs to your neighbor.

And Moses came down from the mountain and told the people what the Lord had said.

Then the Lord called him up onto the mountain again saying, "I will give you tablets of stone on which I have written these commandments."

So Moses went up into the cloud that covered the mountain and he was gone for forty days and forty nights. He was gone for so long that the people were uneasy. They went to Aaron and said, "We do not know what has happened to Moses and we need a god to follow."

Aaron said, "Bring me the gold rings from the ears of your wives, your daughters and your sons."

Then he melted this gold and made from it a statue of a calf. The people said, "This is our god who has brought us out of Egypt."

Aaron built an altar for the calf and proclaimed, "Tomorrow we shall have a festival to honor the Lord."

The next day they all rose early and offered burnt offerings and feasted and danced and sang.

The Lord saw all this and said to Moses, "Go back to your people. Already they have turned away from my commandments. They are worshiping a golden calf. Leave me so that I can destroy them."

But Moses pleaded with God.

"Relent and do not destroy your people," he said. "Remember Abraham, Isaac and Jacob, and remember that you brought us out of Egypt to give us the land that was promised to our fathers."

And God relented and did not punish the people as he had threatened.

Then Moses went down the mountain carrying two tablets of stone with the laws of God written on both sides. And it was God's own writing on the stones.

But when Moses came to the camp and saw the people dancing around the golden calf, he was very angry. He hurled the tablets against the mountain and broke them. He broke the idol, too, and ground it to dust and scattered it on the water and made the people drink the water.

Then he spoke to the people and said, "You have committed a great sin, but I will go again to the Lord and ask him for forgiveness."

Again he went up the mountain and he spoke to God and God spoke with him. And Moses wrote the words of God upon stones. Again he stayed for many days, but this time the people waited. And when Moses came down, they saw that the skin of his face shone because he had been speaking with God. They were afraid to come near him but he put a veil over his face and they listened to him.

He told them that God wanted them to build a beautiful chest of acacia wood and gold to hold the tablets of stone. On their journey they would carry the chest on poles put through rings in its sides. This chest with the tablets in it would be called the ark of the covenant, and it would be the center of worship for the Israelites. When they were camped, the ark would be set in the inner room of a great tent made according to God's plan. The tent would be decorated with gold and silver and bronze and fine cloth given by the people in offering. This tent would be called the tabernacle. And so the ark and the tabernacle were built and dedicated to God with sacrifice and ceremony.

And when Moses went into the inner chamber to speak with the Lord, the presence of the Lord filled the tabernacle. And the Lord said to Moses, "Tell Aaron that this is how he shall bless the children of Israel, 'The Lord bless you and keep you. The Lord make his face to shine upon you and be gracious to you. The Lord turn his face toward you and give you peace.'"

When all had been done as God directed, the children of Israel set out again toward the land of milk and honey. But the way was long and hard and some of the people quarreled and forgot their promises. They grew tired of manna and wished for meat. They were afraid of their enemies and did not believe that the Lord would help and protect them.

The Lord grew angry but he said to Moses, "Your people are my chosen people. I will keep my promise. Descendants of Abraham, Isaac and Jacob will come to the Promised Land. But this generation has complained against me and they have risen up against you, my servant. They will never see the land of milk and honey. They will die in the wilderness. It is their children who will complete the journey. Only Joshua and Caleb, who have been faithful to me, will I bring into the Promised Land."

Now the people came to a desert where there was no water.

They quarreled with Moses and Aaron and said, "Why did you take us out of Egypt and bring us to this place where there is nothing, not even water to drink?"

Moses and Aaron turned away and went to the door of the tabernacle and fell down with their faces to the ground.

The Lord spoke to Moses, "Take the staff and bring the people together before the great rock. Speak to the rock and command it to give up its water. Then all of the Israelites and their animals can drink."

But Moses took the Lord's staff and said to the assembly, "Listen, you quarrelsome people. Shall I make water flow out of this rock?" And he struck the rock twice and water flowed and all could drink.

But the Lord was not pleased. He said to Moses and Aaron, "You did not honor me as I would have you do, but took the power to yourselves. Like the others, you will not enter the Promised Land."

But still Moses led the people for more days and months and years. And then the Lord said to him, "The time is coming when you must die. Call Joshua to come with you into the tabernacle and I will tell him what to do."

When they entered the tent, the Lord appeared in a pillar of cloud and said to Joshua, "Be strong and steadfast. You are the one who will lead the children of Israel into the land that I have promised them. And I shall be there with you."

And to Moses he said, "Go up into the hills of Moab and I will show you the land of Canaan which I will give to the children of Israel." So Moses went up from the valley of the Jordan and climbed to the top of Mount Pisgah.

The Lord said, "I will show you all the land from Gilead to Dan and all of Naphtali and all of Judah, as far as Zoar. This is the land I have promised."

Moses said, "Lord, let me enter that land beyond the Jordan."

But God said, "No! You shall not go in because you did not obey my commandment in the wilderness of Zin. You did not honor me. Your eyes will see this land but you shall not enter."

And Moses died there, in the land of Moab. The children of Israel wept for him in that place for thirty days. And never again has there lived such a prophet with whom the Lord spoke directly, like a man speaking to his friend.

# JOSHUA IN
# THE PROMISED LAND

AFTER THE DEATH of Moses the Lord said to Joshua, "Go and lead the people across the Jordan River into the land that I have promised them. Be strong and have courage, for I am with you wherever you go."

Joshua 1.1-18,
3.1-17, 4.15-24,
5.10-6.20.

Then Joshua commanded the officers of the people to pass through the camp and tell them that in three days they would cross into Canaan, the land they had been seeking for so many years.

The people said to Joshua, "Wherever you send us we will go. We will obey you as we obeyed Moses." And they folded their tents and prepared their provisions.

On the third day, the officers again went through the camp saying, "The priests carrying the ark of the covenant will go before you. Follow the ark, for it will lead you where you are meant to go, but leave a space around the ark. Do not go close to it."

The next day the priests carried the ark to the bank of the Jordan River. Then they did as Joshua had told them to do. They walked into the water. Immediately, the water stopped flowing. The water coming down from above stood still and made a wall of water. The water moving downstream flowed on until it left a wide path of dry earth from one side of the river to the other. The priests walked until they stood in the middle of the river bed. Then they waited while the people of Israel walked across the Jordan on that dry path, making a wide circle around the ark.

When the whole nation of Israel had walked across, the Lord said to Joshua, "Tell the priests to carry the ark up, out of the Jordan." And as soon as the priests stepped on the soil of the Promised Land, the waters returned to their place and the Jordan River flowed as before.

Joshua said to the people, "The Lord parted the waters of the Red Sea for your fathers to cross over. Now he has parted the waters of the Jordan for you so that you could come into the Promised Land knowing that God is with you."

Now the children of Israel camped on the plains of Jericho, and they kept the Passover on the fourteenth day of the month. After the Passover they ate unleavened cakes and parched grain, which were the produce of the land. And from that day on they never again found manna on the ground, but ate the foods grown around them in the fields of Canaan.

Joshua walked out onto the plain to look at the city of Jericho. It was surrounded by high walls and the gates were shut. No one was allowed to go in or out, for the king of Jericho had heard how the Jordan River had stopped flowing to let the Israelites cross over it and he was afraid.

Suddenly a man with a sword in his hand stood before Joshua. Joshua went up to him and said, "Are you for us or are you one of our enemies?"

The man said, "I have come as commander of the army of the Lord."

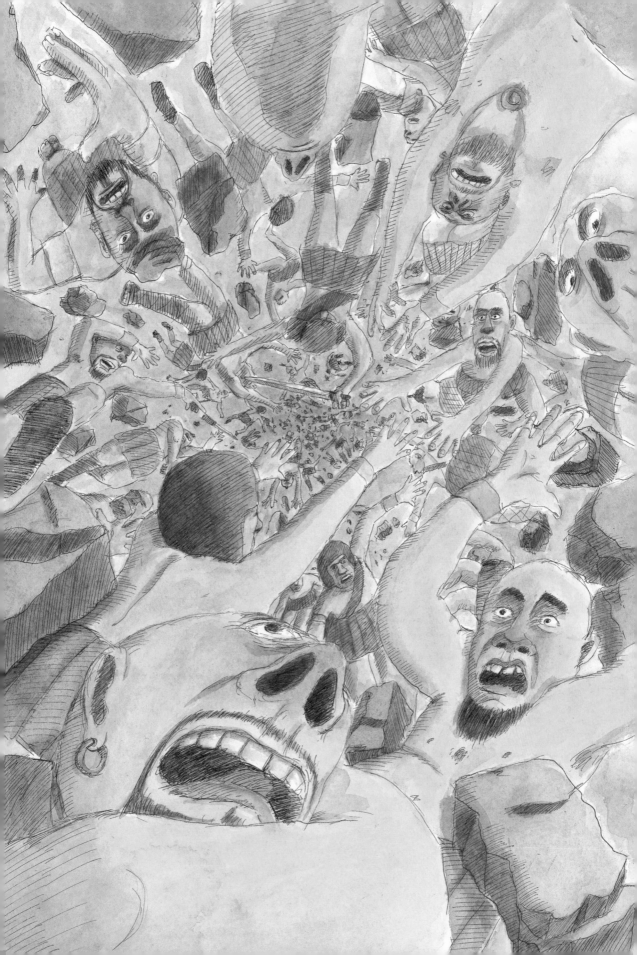

And Joshua fell on his face before him and worshiped him.

And the Lord said to Joshua, "Do as I command you and I will give Jericho to you and your army. It will take seven days." And he told Joshua what must be done.

Joshua went to the people and said, "If we do as the Lord commands, Jericho will be ours." And so the army and all the people prepared themselves.

On the first day Joshua lined up the armed men, followed by seven priests blowing rams' horn trumpets, all going before the ark of the covenant. They marched one time around the walled city with the priests blowing their trumpets. The Israelite people gathered to watch, but Joshua cautioned them not to shout or let any word escape from their mouths. When the army, the priests and the ark of the covenant had circled Jericho, they went back to their camp for the night.

This they did for six days.

On the seventh day, the Israelites rose at dawn. The soldiers armed and arrayed themselves. Then the people watched silently while Joshua led the armed men and the priests blowing their trumpets and the ark of the covenant seven times around the city. When they came before the city gates for the seventh time, they stopped. The priests blew a last long blast on the rams' horn trumpets, and Joshua cried out, "Shout! For the Lord has given us the city of Jericho."

All the children of Israel shouted a great shout. And the walls of the city fell down with a thunderous crash and the Israelite army took Jericho.

# GIDEON

After the time of Joshua, the Israelites often forgot to listen to God and follow the laws of Moses. The tribes became scattered and were easily oppressed by enemies of Israel.

But from time to time, God chose someone wise and good to be a judge over the people and lead them so that they could throw off their oppressors. Ehud was such a judge and so was Deborah, who was called the mother of Israel. Her wisdom led the people to defeat the Canaanites so that there was peace for a generation or more.

Then the Israelites again forgot the teachings of Moses. Many began to worship Baal, one of the gods of Canaan, and they fell into other mistaken ways. And so when the Midianites came raiding, God did not strengthen Israel. The people had to hide in the mountains and in caves while their crops were destroyed and their sheep and cattle stolen away.

After seven years of suffering they remembered that if they lived according to the laws that had been given to Moses, God would help them. So they cried out to God and promised to change. And God heard their prayers.

Gideon was the youngest son of a man called Joash. He had a small plot of land and had managed, in spite of the

Judges 6.1-7.23, 8.22-23.

Midianites, to raise some wheat and harvest it. He took the grain, not to the threshing floor where the enemy would easily see it and steal it from him, but to his wine press, which was hidden under an oak tree.

He was beating the grain with a flail to break the husks when suddenly a stranger, a tall man, appeared beside him and said, "Gideon, the Lord is with you!"

Gideon was tired and discouraged and so he answered, "How can you say that the Lord is with me when my people are threatened on every side and I cannot even thresh my grain in peace?"

The stranger looked him in the eye.

"The Lord is with you," he said again, "and you are a mighty warrior. Now is the time for you to lead your people against the Midianites."

Gideon was astounded.

"How can I do that?" he demanded. "I am not a warrior at all. I am the youngest in my family and my family belongs to the weakest clan in the tribe of Manasseh."

"You will not be alone," said the stranger.

Suddenly Gideon remembered that he must offer hospitality to his guest. He said, "Stay here. I will bring you food."

So he brought meat and bread and broth.

The stranger said, "Put the meat and bread upon this rock and pour the broth over them."

Gideon was puzzled but he did as he was asked. The stranger touched the tip of his staff to the meat and bread. A fire sprang up from the rock and everything Gideon had brought was burnt to nothing. Then the stranger disappeared and Gideon knew that he had been speaking with an angel of God.

He finished his work and went home to his family, but he thought of nothing except what the angel had said. And he was not surprised when, in the night, he heard the voice of God saying, "Your father has built an altar of Baal. Take two of your father's bulls. Use one to pull down the altar. Then offer the second bull as a burnt offering to God."

Gideon took ten men with him and they went out that night and broke the altar and the great image of Baal. Then they made offerings to the God of Israel. When the towns-people came out in the morning and saw the broken idol, they searched and asked questions and came at last to Joash, Gideon's father.

"Give us your son, for he has pulled down the altar to Baal and he must be punished," they said.

Joash was not afraid.

"If Baal is a god, let Baal punish Gideon," he said.

Gideon went on about his work and no harm came to him.

But the Midianites were stronger than ever. Another enemy of Israel, the Amalekites, joined them. A great host with fine weapons and hundreds of swift camels came to raid the territory of the tribe of Manasseh and camped in the val-ley of Jezreel.

When Gideon heard of this, he felt the spirit of God and knew what he must do. He sent messengers into the country-side calling for warriors to join him. Thousands of Israelites came. Some people said that more than thirty thousand were gathered in the camp Gideon had set up to the south of the Midianite army.

Then God said to Gideon, "I do not need so many to fight. When the battle is over everyone must know that the power of God has won the victory."

So Gideon spoke to the throng of Israelites. "If any of you have no heart for this battle, return home now, for God has need of you there."

Great numbers were glad to obey and at last ten thousand remained.

But God said, "Still there are too many. I will tell you what to do."

Gideon listened and then he took all of the men down to the spring to drink. He watched them carefully. Many flung themselves down by the water and lowered their heads and scooped water into their mouths. But a few lapped the water with their tongues so that they could drink and still be watchful. The watchful ones he put aside. There were just three hundred of them. All the others he sent back to their tents.

"With these three hundred I will deliver you," said God.

When night came, Gideon and his chosen men waited in the hills above the camp of the Midianites. They could see hundreds of campfires and hear the clanging of metal and the low voices of thousands of soldiers.

Gideon shook his head. How could his little band of men defeat such a great army? He imagined the soldiers in the valley laughing and singing as they sat around their fires, confident of tomorrow's victory.

"Go and see," said the voice of God.

So Gideon took his servant and they crept down the ridges and ledges of the valley slopes to the edge of the enemy camp. They lay quietly and listened. They heard the Midianite soldiers speaking in whispers about the strength of Gideon and the power of his God.

"He broke the altar to Baal and he lives. They say that the whole of Israel is gathered near, waiting to descend upon us."

One soldier was telling a dream. "I dreamed that a cake of barley bread tumbled into our camp and landed on my tent so that the tent collapsed," he said.

His comrade answered in a low voice, "That was the sword of Gideon, son of Joash. It means that God has given victory into his hand."

Then Gideon was not afraid. He went back to his soldiers and divided them into three companies. He gave each man a ram's horn trumpet and an empty jar with a torch thrust into it.

"Do as I do," he said. "When we come to the outskirts of the camp, I will blow my trumpet. When you hear it, blow your trumpets and shout with great voices, 'For God and for Gideon!'"

They did as Gideon ordered. With the blaring of the trumpets still ringing in the ears of the Midianite army, the Israelites smashed the jars they held and blew their trumpets again. The crashing and blaring echoed from the rocky slopes. Then the men waved the torches and shouted, "A sword for God and for Gideon!"

The Israelites did not move from their places all around the camp, but the noise and the flaring lights terrified the sol-

diers within. They began to run in all directions. When they crashed into each other, they did not know friend from foe. Many killed their own comrades. Others ran from the camp and were caught by Gideon's men. If they got further, the Israelites who had been sent to the tents or those who had returned to their villages pursued them.

At last there were no Midianites left in the land of the tribes of Israel. All the people gave thanks to God for the victory. Then they came to Gideon and said, "Rule over us, for you are great and favored by God."

But Gideon said, "No. I will not rule over you, for it is God who showed us how to win this victory. It is God who truly rules the people of Israel."

And so Gideon became a judge and peace was in the land for many years.

# RUTH AND NAOMI

Ruth 1.1-4.22. THERE WAS A MAN called Elimelech who lived with his wife, Naomi, and their two sons, Mahlon and Chilion, in the town of Bethlehem in Judah. He grew barley and other grains and supported his family well in good years. But a famine came to Judah. No rain fell and the crops withered before he could harvest them.

"I have heard that in the land of Moab there has been rain," Elimelech said to Naomi. "We must go to Moab or we will starve."

And so the family journeyed for many days across the Jordan River and around the Dead Sea to the high plains of Moab where they found good grain ready to harvest.

They settled down and all went well for one year, but then Elimelech died. Naomi grieved but she also gave thanks that in this land, where she was still a stranger, she had two sons to comfort and support her. And so they stayed in Moab. Both sons married young Moabite women. Mahlon's wife was called Ruth and Chilion's was Orpah.

For ten years Naomi and her family lived and worked together. Then suddenly both Mahlon and Chilion died.

Naomi knew that Ruth and Orpah loved her dearly, but she also knew how hard the lives of three women alone would be.

One day in the marketplace she chanced to hear news that the famine in Judah was over and that there were good harvests.

"I must return to Judah," she said to Ruth and Orpah. "My life here is over. You have been kind to me and to my sons, and I pray that God will be kind to you. It will be best for you to return to your mothers' houses. You are young. Perhaps you will find security with new husbands. I cannot give you either security or husbands, for I have no more sons."

Orpah kissed Naomi and wept. Then she prepared to return to her old home. But Ruth could not say goodbye to Naomi. She put her arms around her and said, "Don't ask me to leave you. Where you go, I will go. Where you live, I will live. Your people will become my people and I will worship God as you do."

Naomi saw that Ruth was determined and perhaps she was glad, for she said no more about it and the two women set out for Judah.

They traveled for many days and at last reached Bethlehem. As they walked through the streets of the town, the women who had gathered at the well in the evening stared at Naomi.

"Is that you, Naomi?" they asked in amazement. "You have changed in these years."

"It is I," said Naomi, "and I have changed, for my life has been sad. I left Bethlehem with my husband and two sons. Now they are all dead. Only my daughter-in-law has returned with me."

Naomi and Ruth settled in a little house together. It was the time of the barley harvest but they had no crops of their

own to bring in. Ruth tried to think of a way to get food for the two of them for the coming winter.

"When the barley is cut," she said to Naomi, "could I go along behind the reapers and pick up the stalks of grain that they leave behind?"

Naomi nodded. "It has always been the custom to allow gleaners to gather behind the reapers. Go, my daughter, for we must find food for ourselves."

As Ruth set about gleaning the grain that had fallen, she chanced to go into a field that belonged to Boaz. He was a wealthy man who was of the same family as Elimelech. Boaz noticed Ruth and said to the servant who was in charge of the reapers, "Who is that young woman? I have not seen her before."

"She is the one who came with Naomi from Moab," answered the servant. "She asked for permission to glean after the reapers, and she has worked without stopping since early this morning. I think that she and Naomi are sorely in need of food."

Then Boaz said to Ruth, "You are welcome to glean in this field, and there is no need for you to go to any other. I will see that no one bothers you. And when you are thirsty, go and drink from the water my young men have drawn."

Ruth fell before Boaz and thanked him.

"Why are you being so kind to me, a foreigner?" she asked.

"I have heard of how your father-in-law and your own husband died and how you have cared for Naomi. You have even come with her to live among strangers. These are good deeds."

When it came time for the reapers to eat, Boaz made sure

that Ruth sat with them and shared their bread. He heaped parched grain before her. When the meal was over he gave her more bread to take home to Naomi and he said to his reapers, "Take some grain from your bundles and leave it in the way of the Moabite woman." And so Ruth came home with plenty of grain to store for the winter.

Naomi was pleased but she was still troubled. The grain would keep them from starvation, but she knew that life would always be hard for the two of them alone. They needed to be part of a household. It would be best for Ruth to marry. She would not leave Naomi. She had promised. Just as Ruth had come with her, so Naomi would go with Ruth.

Now she said to Ruth, "You have done well. Where did you glean today? I bless the owner of that field, for he has been kind."

"The field is owned by Boaz," said Ruth, "and he is indeed kind, for he gave me food and water and made sure that I gathered all of this barley."

Naomi was filled with joy. "Blessed be the name of God whose kindness has not forsaken us after all," she said. "Boaz is near kin to my husband. He has shown that he will not leave us in misery."

As the barley and wheat harvest went on, Naomi became sure that Boaz' kindness to Ruth meant that he liked her and thought well of her.

One afternoon she said to Ruth, "Tonight Boaz will be watching over the winnowing of the barley. He will sleep on the threshing floor to guard the grain. Wash yourself and put on your best clothes and go to him."

Ruth did as Naomi told her to do. She went to Boaz as he lay by the heaped-up barley. When he saw her, she said, "I have come to you, for through my father-in-law, you are my near kinsman."

He was pleased and answered, "I am glad you have come. I know, and all of my people know, that you are a worthy woman. I will tell the elders of the town that I wish to act as next of kin to you. It is the custom for kin to take care of kin."

Ruth knew that this was a promise. Then Boaz gave her six measures of barley to take to Naomi. When Naomi saw the barley and heard what Boaz had said, she was content.

"He will settle the matter today," she said. "His mind is made up."

Boaz spoke to the elders and to the near kin of Elimelech. They all agreed that he should take on the inheritance and responsibilities that had come to Naomi, and that Ruth should be his wife.

All happened as Naomi and Ruth and Boaz wanted it to. Ruth and Boaz were married. And in time Ruth gave birth to a son, named Obed, who became the father of Jesse who became the father of David, the great king of Israel.

And Naomi in her old age was content. As the women of Bethlehem said to her, "God has given you a grandson to care for you and a daughter-in-law who has loved you so well that she is more to you than seven sons might be. Blessed be the Lord."

# SAMUEL, SAUL AND DAVID

I Samuel 8.4-10.1,
15.10-16.13.

SAMUEL WAS DEDICATED to the Lord from childhood and became a wise judge over the people. When he was old, and the time had come for a new leader to be named, the elders of Israel decided that for the first time the nation of Israel, like other nations, should be ruled by a king. They asked Samuel to choose a man to be king over the Israelites and lead them in battle. At first Samuel refused but then the Lord said to him, "Listen to the voice of the people in this matter." And in the end, Samuel agreed.

Now there was a man of the tribe of Benjamin called Kish, and his son Saul was a tall and handsome young man. One day Saul went to bring his father's donkeys from the place where they were stabled, but the donkeys were gone. Kish said to Saul, "Take one of the servants and go and look for the beasts."

The two men set out and searched the hill country and all through the lands of the tribe of Benjamin, but they found no donkeys. When they came to the land of Zuph, Saul said, "We should turn back, for my father may be anxious about us."

But the servant said, "There is a man in this city who is honored because all that he says comes true. Perhaps he can help us find the donkeys."

[138]

Now this man was Samuel. The day before, God had spoken to him and said, "Tomorrow a man will come to you from the land of Benjamin, and I want you to anoint him to be king over all my people. For I have heard my people cry out to me because they are beset by the Philistines."

When Samuel saw Saul coming toward him, he knew that this was the man God had chosen. He said to Saul, "I am the one you are looking for and, as for your donkeys, seek them no longer for they are found."

Then Samuel set Saul in a high place at his table and honored him. In the morning he took the young man aside. He poured a vial of oil upon his head and kissed him and said, "The Lord has chosen you to be king over the people of Israel."

So Saul became king. He led his people in many battles and strove fiercely for them. But he also forgot God and did not always obey his commandments.

At last God spoke to Samuel and said, "I have rejected Saul. He is not worthy to be king and I have found a successor who will be worthy. Go to Jesse of Bethlehem. He has eight sons and I will show you the one I have chosen."

So Samuel went to Jesse and said, "Gather together all of your sons." Seven young men came at their father's bidding.

One by one each of them stood before Samuel though they did not know why. First came Eliab. Samuel looked at his fine appearance and thought, "Surely he is the one." But the Lord said to Samuel, "Pay no attention to his face and stature. He is not the one, for I look only at the heart."

Then Jesse called Abinadab, but the Lord said, "He is not

the one." And then Shammah, but the Lord again said, "He is not the one." And so seven sons of Jesse passed before Samuel but the Lord did not choose any of them.

"Are all of your sons here?" Samuel asked.

"There is David, the youngest. He is tending the sheep," answered Jesse.

He sent a servant to run and tell David to come to him.

"Is my father taken sick?" asked David, a little worried. He had never been called in from the hills before.

"No, he is well. He is gathered with all of your brothers. And Samuel is there, he who used to be judge over Israel before Saul became king. Don't stand and stare at me. Be off!"

David ran. But before he came into the house, he paused to catch his breath. It would not do honor to Samuel to come before him gasping and panting. He found his brothers and his father standing around an old man who also stood, holding a traveling staff firmly planted in the dirt floor. They were all silent, waiting for him.

"David, my son, the prophet Samuel has asked to see you," said Jesse.

David knelt before Samuel but when he raised his eyes, he saw that the old man was not looking at him. He seemed to be listening.

David listened, too, but he heard nothing.

Suddenly Samuel looked into his eyes for a long moment. Then he said, "Rise, David, son of Jesse. The Lord has told me that you will be the king of Israel after Saul. I am to anoint you." From his belt he took a horn of oil and poured a measure of it on David's head.

David heard Samuel's words but he wondered how they could be true. He was the youngest son of a farmer. But Saul, too, came from a humble family and Saul, too, had been anointed by Samuel. Suddenly David was not afraid. He knew that in time God would help him to do what he must do.

Samuel smiled. "The spirit of God is with you, my son," he said. "I can see it in your face. Now you must return to your sheep and I must go on my way."

David did as Samuel said. He returned to the flock. But now he had something to think about beyond Bethlehem and the hills. Still, he was young and Saul would be king for many years.

# DAVID AND GOLIATH

WHILE SAUL RULED as king of Israel, David spent I Samuel 16.14-17.51. his days watching his father's sheep in the hills near Bethlehem. His seven older brothers and his father, Jesse, were all busy with sowing and reaping and taking grain and wool to market. So David was left to watch over the flocks alone.

To pass the time, David carried with him a small harp called a lyre. He learned to play it with great skill, and sometimes he made up songs that pleased him and the sheep. But even when the music was sweetest, David had to keep his wits about him. In that wild hill country there were lions and bears that would gladly make off with a sheep or a lamb. He learned that by being quick and fearless and by using the stones that lay to hand, he could keep the sheep safe.

King Saul knew nothing of David. He was a warrior king who defended the tribes of Israel against surrounding peoples. He was a great leader but a troubled man. He had known since he became king that he had been chosen by God to bring all the tribes of Israel together. But now he had lost his way. Instead of doing as God wished and destroying all the goods his army had captured, Saul had become greedy, keeping riches for himself and the leaders of his army. Because of this, God had abandoned him. Saul could not sleep and his thoughts were dark.

His servants said, "Perhaps music would calm you. Then you could sleep and peace would come to you."

"Do you know of someone who plays well upon the lyre?' said Saul. "That music would please me."

One of the young men said, "I have seen a son of Jesse of Bethlehem who plays well and is also a brave man. They say the Lord is with him."

So Saul sent for David, and David came with gifts from his father – bread and wine and a young kid. He brought his lyre, of course, and whenever the dark mood came over the king, David played for him. Saul listened and the music soothed him and lifted his spirits. And so he loved David and took him into his service.

But the king could not rest long. The Philistines came from the south with a great army and made camp above the valley of Elah, near Bethlehem. The army of Israel gathered on the other side of the valley, with the king to lead them. David's three oldest brothers were in that army, and so David went back to his father who needed him to guard the sheep.

The Philistines were great warriors with weapons of iron that easily pierced the armor and shields used by the Israelites. They were a mighty and terrifying army. But they were invaders and Saul's army would fight on its own ground. So rather than engage the Israelites in battle immediately, the Philistines taunted them.

They had in their army a giant of a man, taller than any Israelite. Saul himself, though he stood head and shoulders above any of his own men, could barely have reached his hand to the top of the head of this Philistine, who was called Goliath of Gath.

Goliath was not only tall, but mighty, with a voice that boomed across the valley. Every day he strode out from the Philistine camp, clad in full bronze armor and bearing a great spear with a heavy iron tip. He stood and shouted across the valley, "If you have a true warrior among you, send him out. If he fights me and kills me, then my people will be your servants. But if I kill him, then all of you Israelites will serve the Philistines. I challenge you to send someone to fight me."

But Saul and all his soldiers were afraid. Not one of them dared to take up Goliath's challenge. For fifty days they stayed in their camp, looking across the valley and listening to the taunts.

One day Jesse sent David to the Israelite camp to take his brothers some food – a sack of parched barley and ten loaves of bread. "And take these ten cheeses to their commander," he said. "Look about you and bring back news."

When David came to the encampment, he saw that the army was making ready to form a battle line. Weapons were clanging and men were shouting. He left the supplies with the man in charge of baggage and ran to greet his brothers in the ranks. He could see the Philistine army lined up on the other side of the valley. As David talked to his brothers all the men suddenly fell silent. Goliath was striding out from the Philistine line.

David watched him as he came to the edge of the little stream that flowed through the valley. The sun glittered on his bronze armor and David squinted so that he could see clearly. Truly, this giant man was covered in metal — his body, his arms, his legs. The armor must have weighed as much as a pile of rocks. No wonder Goliath did not carry his shield himself. Instead, a shield bearer walked beside him carrying a great bronze shield.

David could not see much of Goliath's face. His helmet curved around and covered his temples and his cheeks. But David could see the gleam of his eyes.

Just then Goliath opened his great mouth and bellowed his challenge. The Israelites looked at each other in despair. Not one of them dared to fight this monstrous man and yet, if they abandoned their position, the Philistine army would march across the valley and into their land.

David was outraged. "Who is this barbarian who defies the army of God's people?" he demanded. "Can no one kill this Philistine and take away dishonor from Israel? What would happen to the man who did this deed?"

The soldiers shrugged their shoulders. "Of course the king would reward him," said one. "He would give him his daughter as a wife and raise up his family in honor."

David's oldest brother, Eliab, heard his young brother talking and came over.

"Why are you saying such foolish things? You are just a young troublemaker wanting to see the battle. Go back to those few sheep you guard in the wilderness."

"I was only asking questions," said David. He turned away from Eliab and joined another group of soldiers and asked the questions again.

Soon word of David's questions reached Saul. He immediately had David brought to his tent.

"What is the use of asking these questions?" he said. "We have been here for fifty days, and no one has come forward to kill this giant and save Israel. I know now that no one will."

"Do not say so," said David. He stood straight and looked at his king fearlessly. "I will fight him."

Saul stared. "You are only a boy," he said at last. "This man has been a warrior from his youth. It is senseless for you to go against him."

But David answered, "I have been a shepherd for my father and whenever a lion or a bear comes to take a lamb from the flock, I strike it down. If a lion has a lamb in its mouth, I catch it by the jaw and save the lamb and kill the lion. God, who has saved me from the claws of bears and lions, will save me from the hand of this Philistine."

"Very well," said Saul. "May God be with you. I will give you armor and weapons."

David put on Saul's own armor and strapped on Saul's sword. But the armor was clumsy and the sword heavy.

"I cannot walk in this armor," he said. "How would I fight? And I do not need the sword. I have a weapon of my own."

So David took off the armor and picked up his sling. It was made of leather and shaped to hold a smooth stone the size of an egg. In his years with the sheep, David had learned how to whirl the sling on its leather thongs and let go at the right moment so that the stone flew through the air at great speed. He had learned to hit a small target, very far away. He knew what his target was now.

David took his shepherd's staff and walked down to the stream. He carefully chose five stones and put them in his pouch. Then he walked along the stream until he came near to Goliath who was still roaring at the Israelites. When Goliath saw David he was quiet for a minute, staring. Then he laughed.

"Am I a dog that you come at me with a stick?" he said. "I curse you and I will give your flesh to the birds of the air and the wild animals to eat."

David was not afraid.

"You come to me with sword and spear," he said. "I come to you in the name of the God of Israel. He will deliver you into my hand and into the hand of Israel."

Goliath stood his ground defiantly but David came toward him quickly. As he ran he cast down his staff and took a stone from his pouch. He fitted it into the sling and spun the sling around and around his head. He fixed his eyes on Goliath's eyes and let go. The stone flew through the air and struck the giant in the spot David had marked in his mind – the center of Goliath's forehead, just above his eyes.

Goliath fell. He crashed face down onto the ground and David picked up the heavy sword that fell beside him. Swinging it with both hands he struck off Goliath's head.

The Philistine army fled and David went no more to watch over his father's sheep. He became a captain in the army of Israel.

# DAVID AND SOLOMON
# BUILD JERUSALEM

WHEN SAUL DIED David became king of Israel. He had waited a long time, sometimes hiding in the wilderness, sometimes leading the army of Israel, because Saul, in his troubled mind, changed between fearing David and loving him.

David brought the people of Judah in the south and the tribes of Israel in the north together to be one nation called Israel. And now this nation needed a city that belonged not to one tribe but to all twelve tribes equally.

Jerusalem was the last city held by the Canaanites. David looked at it from afar. It was built on a hill, and it lay between the territories of the northern tribes and the southern tribes of Israel. It had two good springs of water and was on the trade routes to the sea. David decided that Jerusalem would make a very good capital city for his people. And with the strong army of Israel, he captured Jerusalem easily.

The king of Tyre, a country that lay by the sea to the north of Israel, heard of King David and his new capital city. He sent fine cedar trees to be used to build a house for David, and he sent craftsmen to make the house beautiful. David was honored but he wanted more for Jerusalem. He wanted to build a temple where all the people of Israel could feel the presence of God.

I Samuel 18.1-16;
II Samuel 5.1-12,
6.1-7.17;
I Kings 2.10-12,
3.5-29, 5.1-8.11,
10.1-13.

First he must bring the ark of the covenant to Jerusalem. This holy chest contained the stone tablets of the laws that God had given to Moses. It had been carried from place to place for three hundred years and more. For a time it had even been captured by the Philistines. Now David wished to build the ark of the covenant a worthy home.

He chose thirty thousand men and went to the place where the ark was kept in a small tent. They put it on a newly built cart and brought it into Jerusalem with the sound of trumpets. David himself and all the house of Israel danced before the ark with songs and the music of harps and tambourines and castanets and cymbals, as it was carried through the streets to the fine tent that had been prepared for it. There David made offerings and said prayers for Jerusalem, the holy city. And he gave gifts of bread and meat and raisins to all the people.

David settled in his beautiful house, and the Lord gave him rest from the enemies that surrounded his land. But David thought, "Here I am, living in a house of cedar while the ark of God still stays in a tent. It is time for me to build a temple for the Lord."

Then God spoke to the prophet Nathan and said, "Tell David I have lived in a tent since I brought the people out of Egypt. I have not asked for a house of cedar. Your work is to establish the kingdom of my people Israel. In later years your offspring will build a house for me."

So David did not build a temple. Instead he fought many difficult battles to preserve Israel and make it strong, and he had many children. When he died, his son Solomon inherited a peaceful kingdom. He was a man who loved God and respected the ways of his father, David.

Soon after Solomon became king, God appeared to him in a dream and said, "Ask me for what I should give you." In the dream Solomon said to God, "You showed steadfast love for my father, David, who was a great king because he was faithful to you. I do not know how to be a good king, so I ask for an understanding mind that I may know how to govern your great people."

God was pleased by this answer and said, "Because you have asked for wisdom rather than for riches or long life, I will give you all three."

Soon afterward two women came before King Solomon with a dispute. They both lived in the same house and each had given birth to a baby. But one baby had died and now each woman claimed the living baby as her own. Solomon looked at the two women and at the baby and called for his sword to be brought. Then he said, "Cut this child in two pieces. Then each woman can have half of a child."

One of the women stepped forward quickly and said, "Please, my lord, give her the baby. I would rather lose him than have him killed."

Solomon spoke to the other woman, "And what do you say?"

She said, "The baby shall be neither mine nor hers. Divide it."

Then the king said, "Give the child to the woman who would have him live. She is the true mother."

All Israel heard of this judgment by the king and the story

traveled even to foreign lands. Everyone marveled at the wisdom of Solomon. And indeed, as time passed, people came from all nations to hear him speak. He composed proverbs and songs and knew much of trees and animals and birds and fish and reptiles.

Now King Solomon set about building the temple that his father, David, had dreamed of. He sent to King Hiram of Tyre for cedar, and he conscripted workers from all Israel to cut stone in the hill country and prepare timber of all kinds. The temple took seven years to build and it was grand and beautiful. In front of it stood a great bronze basin held on the backs of twelve carved oxen. The doors and the walls inside were lined with polished wood and decorated with carvings and with gold. The inner room, the holy of holies where the ark of the covenant would dwell, was lined with pure gold but it was as dark as night, for as God wished, it had no windows.

When the temple was ready, Solomon ordered a great ceremony of dedication. Countless sacrifices were made and the priests brought the ark of the covenant into the inner room. When it was put in its place and the doors were closed, a dazzling light filled the great chamber. All who were there felt the presence of God.

Now Solomon built himself a great palace and he had walls built around the whole city. And news of the wonders of Jerusalem spread abroad over the world.

Even the queen of Sheba heard of Solomon's wisdom and wealth, and she traveled to Jerusalem to test him with hard questions. She came with a great retinue of serving men and women, and with camels loaded with gold and precious stones and spices. When the king had spoken with her and answered all her questions, and when she had seen the beauty of his house and city, she said to him, "I did not believe the stories of your wisdom and prosperity. Now I see they are all true. Blessed be your God for he has set you to rule Israel with justice and righteousness." Then she gave him the gifts that she had brought and he gave fine gifts to her out of his royal bounty. And then the queen and all her people returned to Sheba.

So Solomon ruled in Jerusalem, the city he and his father had built for Israel and for the glory of God, the golden city of David, set upon a hill.

# ELIJAH

AFTER THE TIME of Solomon, the kingdom of Israel broke again into two parts, Israel in the north and Judah in the south. The kings who ruled both lands believed that they followed the God of Israel but many did not remember his teachings. In time a king called Ahab took the throne of Israel, and he did more to anger God than had all the kings who came before him. Although he worshiped the Lord himself, he built a great temple to Baal, the Canaanite god of rain and the growth of crops, at Samaria. His wife, Jezebel, was a Phoenician who worshiped Baal and drove many prophets of the Lord into hiding or had them killed.

One day a man called Elijah came into Ahab's court and announced, "As the God of Israel lives, there shall be neither rain nor dew in this land, except by my word."

Ahab was amazed that an ordinary man would speak so boldly to his king. Jezebel was enraged because Elijah was declaring that he had more power than Baal.

But before they could order the guards to seize the prophet, God spoke to him and said, "Go away from this place. Go to the stream called Cherith, east of the Jordan." Elijah went immediately and Ahab did not know where he had gone.

I Kings 16.29-19.21; II Kings 2.1-15.

[*157*]

Elijah found himself in a barren place. But God sent ravens carrying bread and meat for him in the morning and the evening, and he drank water from the stream. So Elijah fared well until the drought he had foretold caused the stream to dry up.

Then God spoke to him again and said, "Go to the town of Zarephath in Jezebel's homeland. I have commanded a widow there to feed you."

So Elijah set out for Zarephath and found a Canaanite widow gathering sticks near the town gate.

"Could you give me a little water to drink and a morsel of bread to eat?" he said to her.

"I can give you water," she said. "But I have no bread, only a handful of flour and a drop of oil. I am gathering sticks so that I can build a fire. I will mix up a little dough and bake it to share with my son. Then we will die, for we have no more to eat."

Elijah said to her, "Do not be afraid. Make me a little cake out of the flour you have and bring it to me. Afterward you can make bread for yourself and your son, for the God of Israel says that until he sends rain, your flour jar will not be empty and your oil jug will not be dry."

The widow did as Elijah asked, and she and her son and Elijah ate for many weeks of the flour and oil the Lord provided.

In the third year of the drought, God sent Elijah back to confront Ahab again. The king was not pleased to see him.

"Is that you, you troubler of Israel?" he asked.

"You are the troubler of Israel because you have forsaken the commandments of the Lord. Now, gather the people at Mount Carmel, overlooking the sea, where there is an altar to

Baal. Bring the four hundred and fifty priests of Baal who eat at Jezebel's table, and bring two fine bulls. The priests will choose one bull and prepare it for sacrifice. I will prepare the other. We will each call upon our god. Whichever god answers with fire and burns the sacrifice is the true God."

Ahab gathered a great crowd of Israelites and hundreds of priests of Baal.

Elijah said to the people, "You cannot continue to divide yourselves between two gods. We will see here whether Baal or the God of Israel is the true god." And the people agreed.

The priests prepared their bull and called on Baal all morning, until noon. They called and danced until they were hoarse and limping.

Elijah laughed at them.

"You must cry louder! Perhaps your god is meditating or he is on a journey or asleep. Shout again!"

But no matter how they shouted and cried out to Baal, nothing happened. The offering lay upon the altar.

Then Elijah said to the people, "Come near." And the people came close to him. He took twelve stones and used them to repair an old altar to God that had been destroyed. "Each of these stones is one of the tribes of Israel," he said. "See how together they make a strong altar in the name of the Lord."

Next he laid wood upon the altar and arranged the offering upon it. Then he dug a trench around it. He asked the people to fill jars with water and pour it over the wood. They did this until the wood was soaked and the trench was filled with water.

Then Elijah went to the altar alone and prayed, "O God of

STORIES FROM ADAM AND EVE TO EZEKIEL

Abraham, Isaac and Jacob, answer me so that the people of Israel will know that you are God." When he had spoken, fire fell from heaven upon the altar and consumed everything — the offering, the wood, the stones and even the water in the trench.

Seeing this the people fell on their faces and worshiped God. Elijah said, "Rise up and seize these prophets of Baal, for they have been defeated in a holy war and they must die." So hundreds of prophets of Baal were killed.

Then Elijah said to Ahab, "Though the sun still beats down upon us, I hear the sound of rain coming." Then he went to the top of Mount Carmel and bowed down and prayed to God. Seven times he said to his servant, "Look out to sea. Do you see anything in the sky?"

Six times the servant said, "There is nothing." But the seventh time he turned to Elijah and said, "Look, there is a little cloud no bigger than my hand rising out of the sea."

Elijah lifted his head and said, "Go to Ahab. Tell him to harness his chariot and go to his palace before the storm stops him. The drought is broken!"

Ahab told Jezebel that Elijah had defeated the priests of Baal and had killed them afterward and she was filled with anger. She swore that she would find the prophet and see him executed. So once again Elijah had to flee. He went through Judah to Beersheba and on alone into the Sinai desert.

He sat down under a solitary broom tree, so discouraged that he asked God if he might die. "I have done no good," he said. "So what good is my life?" Then he lay down and fell asleep.

He was awakened by an angel who touched him and said, "Get up and eat." He looked and there beside him was a cake baked on hot stones and a jar of water. He ate and drank, then he fell asleep again.

After a time the angel awakened him again and said, "Get up and eat, otherwise you will not have strength for your journey."

So Elijah ate and drank, and the food and water gave him such strength that he walked for forty days and forty nights until he came to Mount Sinai. There he found a cave where he spent the night.

In the morning the word of God came to him. "What are you doing here, Elijah?"

He answered, "I have worked and struggled for the Lord, but the Israelites have not kept the covenant they made with him. I am all alone and they are searching for me to take my life."

The voice spoke again, "Go out and stand upon the mountain for the Lord is about to pass by."

Elijah obeyed and as he stood there a great wind came, so strong that it cracked the rocks of the mountain. But Elijah knew that the Lord was not in the wind. Next an earthquake shook the earth under Elijah's feet, but he knew that the Lord was not in the earthquake. Then a fire swept past him, but he knew that the Lord was not in the fire, either.

After the fire was gone, complete silence fell over the mountain. Elijah listened to that silence and out of it came a small, quiet voice that said, "What are you doing here, Elijah?"

And Elijah said again, "I have worked and struggled for the

Lord, but the Israelites have not kept the covenant they made with him and they are searching for me to take my life."

But God said, "You must return to your land. You will find Elisha of Abel-meholah and anoint him prophet to take your place when your time is done. Remember there are people in Israel who have not bowed to Baal."

So Elijah took heart and returned to Israel. He found Elisha, son of Shaphat, and Elisha followed him. Together they struggled with the forces of Baal and the blindness of the people of Israel.

At last a day came when Elijah knew that God had a plan for the end of his life on earth. He was with Elisha traveling from Gilgal toward Bethel and he said to him, "Stay here and I will go on."

But Elisha said, "As the Lord lives and as you live, I will not leave you."

When they got to Bethel a company of prophets came up and said to Elisha, "Do you know that today the Lord will take your master away from you?"

"Yes, I know," said Elisha, "but don't speak of it."

Elijah said, "Stay here, Elisha, for the Lord has sent me on to Jericho."

But Elisha said, "As the Lord lives and as you live, I will not leave you."

At Jericho some prophets said, "Do you know that today is the day the Lord will take your master away from you?"

"Yes, I know," said Elisha, "but don't speak of it."

Then Elijah said to him, "Stay here, for the Lord has sent me to the Jordan River."

But Elisha said, "As the Lord lives, and as you live, I will not leave you."

So they went on together and fifty prophets also went behind them. When they got to the river, Elijah took his mantle and rolled it up and struck the water with it. The water parted so that the two of them could walk across on dry land. Then it flowed as a river again.

When they were on the other side, Elijah said to Elisha, "Tell me, what I can do for you before I am taken away?"

"Let me inherit a double share of your spirit," said Elisha.

"That is a hard thing," said Elijah. "But if you can see me as I am being taken away from you, you will know that your wish has been granted. If you cannot see me, it will not be done."

They went on walking and talking. Then suddenly a chariot of fire pulled by horses of fire came between Elijah and Elisha. Elisha saw a whirlwind lift Elijah in the chariot up toward heaven. When he could no longer see the flames of the chariot, he grasped his own robe and tore it into two pieces.

Then he looked on the ground and saw Elijah's mantle lying there. He picked it up and went back to the Jordan. He rolled the mantle up, just as Elijah had done, and struck the water with it, and the water parted so that he could cross.

The prophets who were waiting saw him coming and said, "Now the spirit of the prophet Elijah rests on Elisha."

# JONAH AND THE
# GREAT FISH

Jonah 1.1-4.11.

THE LORD SPOKE to a prophet named Jonah and said, "I have heard of the wickedness of the great Assyrian city of Nineveh. I want you to go and speak to the people there and turn them to my ways."

But Jonah did not want to go to Nineveh because the people there were enemies of his people, the Israelites. He did not want them to follow the ways of the Lord and be forgiven for their sins. So he went to Joppa and found a ship going to Tarshish, hoping that the Lord would not find him there.

But as soon as the ship was away from the harbor, the Lord sent a strong wind that stirred up a great storm. The ship shook and creaked and the sailors cried out to their gods. They threw cargo overboard to lighten the ship for they were afraid it would break up and sink.

The captain went to look for Jonah and found him fast asleep below deck.

"Wake up!" he shouted. "How can you sleep? Come up and call upon your god! Perhaps he will save us from drowning."

But the sailors looked at Jonah and said, "Someone is causing this disaster to happen to us. Quickly! We must cast lots and see who is to blame." And when they cast lots, the lot fell to Jonah.

"Who are you?" they said. "Where do you come from and what sort of man are you? Who are your people?"

Jonah answered, "I am a Hebrew and I honor the Lord who made the sea and the land."

The men looked at him with fear and said, "What have you done to make your god angry? And what can we do to calm the sea?"

"Throw me into the sea and the storm will stop," said Jonah. "I know that I am bringing this danger upon you all."

But the sailors did not want to throw Jonah into the sea. They rowed as hard as they could to bring the ship toward land but the waves grew higher and they could not get it to safety. So they cried out, "O Lord, we beg that you do not let us perish because of this man's error and we pray that you will not blame us for his death, for it was you who sent the storm that threatens us."

Then they picked up Jonah and threw him into the sea and at once it became calm. Then the sailors were even more frightened and they offered a sacrifice to the Lord.

Jonah, however, did not perish. The Lord sent a great fish to swallow him into its belly and there he stayed for three days and three nights. And Jonah prayed to the Lord from the belly of the fish in the hope that he would be saved:

> Out of my distress I called to the Lord,
> and you answered me.
> From the place of darkness I cried,
> and you heard me.
> For you did throw me into the heart of the sea,
> and the water is around me,

and the waves pass over me.

Yet you brought back my life.

I speak with the voice of thanksgiving.

Then the Lord spoke to the fish and caused it to spit Jonah out upon dry land. And as Jonah sat on the shore of the sea, the word of the Lord came to him again. "Go to Nineveh and give the people the message I will give to you."

So Jonah went to Nineveh. He found a city so large it would take three days to walk across it, but he went one day's journey into the heart of the city and began to speak to the people.

"Because of your wickedness," he cried, "the city will be destroyed in forty days."

And the people believed the word of God that he was giving them. All of them, from the king to the least beggar in the streets, began to fast and put on sackcloth as a sign that they repented their evil ways. Even the beasts wore sackcloth.

The Lord saw that the people were listening to his word and honoring him, and he knew that they truly repented the evil they had done. So he did not punish them by destroying the city.

Jonah was not pleased by this. It seemed that his prophecy to the people of Nineveh would not be fulfilled. He prayed to God, "I fled from you because I know that you are a gracious and merciful God. You are full of love and slow to carry out judgment. The people of Nineveh were wicked but you will not punish them. I have made a prophecy but it will not come true. It would be better for me to die than to live and I ask you to take my life."

But the Lord only asked, "Are you right to be angry?"

Jonah left Nineveh and went to the east and set up a little shelter in a place where he had a good view of the city. And there he sat watching to see whether the Lord would punish Nineveh.

God caused a vine to grow up over Jonah's shelter to make a cooler, shadier place for him to sit. Jonah was pleased with the vine. Then God sent a worm that attacked the vine and caused it to wither. And afterward he sent a warm, wet wind and the sun to beat upon Jonah's head.

Jonah was hot and faint. He said to God, "Now you should surely let me die for the vine that sheltered me has died."

God asked, "Is it right that you be angry that the plant is gone?"

And Jonah said, "Yes, it is right."

And God said, "You care about the plant because it is dead, even though you did nothing to make it grow. So why should I not care about the people of Nineveh, one hundred and twenty thousand of them, whose spirits were dying because of the evil they did. They have repented and come to me, and so I will not punish them."

And so Jonah, who had himself been forgiven by God, had to learn that others would be forgiven, too.

# DANIEL IN THE LION'S DEN

MANY GENERATIONS OF KINGS ruled over Judah, but as time passed, they forgot the laws given to Moses and no longer followed them. The Lord grew angry and turned his face away from the Israelites. King Nebuchadnezzar of Babylon invaded Judah and Jerusalem fell. Many Israelites were taken away into servitude.

II Kings 24.1-5; Daniel 1.1-6, 6.1-24.

One of these was a young man called Daniel who had been brought up to honor and obey the Lord. He was well educated and capable and he quickly learned the ways of the Babylonian court. Nebuchadnezzar and the kings that followed him put Daniel into positions of power and trust, even though he continued to worship God as he had been taught.

When Darius the Mede became king of Babylon, he made Daniel one of his three chief ministers. Because of his abilities Daniel far outshone the other two ministers, and the king decided to make him the grand vizier with authority over all the ministers, prefects, satraps, courtiers and viceroys.

When word of Daniel's appointment came to these officials, they were not at all pleased. They began to plot against Daniel. First they looked for some corruption or neglect of duty they could blame on him, but Daniel was faithful to his trust and they could find nothing. So they began to look for something in his practice of religion that they could use against him with the king.

At last they all went together to Darius and said, "Long live the king. All of us — ministers, prefects, satraps, courtiers and viceroys — have agreed that you, O King, are the greatest in the land, and that you should issue a decree saying that for the next thirty days no one may offer a petition to anyone but you, be it god or man. Anyone who disobeys this decree will be thrown into a den of lions. Issue this decree in writing, O King, and all must obey it, for it is known that the law of the Medes and the Persians may not be changed."

The king, thinking only that they sought to honor him, issued the decree.

As soon as Daniel heard what the king had done he went to the upper room in his house. There he had windows facing toward Jerusalem and on this day, as on all other days, Daniel knelt and offered prayers and praises to his God.

His enemies were watching and when they saw him praying they went to the king.

"You have issued a decree that any person who presents a petition to anyone but you in these thirty days will be thrown into a den of lions. Daniel, one of the exiles of Judah, has been making petitions to his God. He has not obeyed your decree."

King Darius was greatly troubled and tried to think of a way to save Daniel. All day he struggled but at sunset, when Daniel's enemies came to him again, he had thought of nothing.

"We remind you, O King," they said, "that by the law of the Medes and the Persians, your decree must be obeyed and cannot be changed."

So the king ordered that Daniel be brought to the place where the lions were kept in a pit. As the guards were thrusting their prisoner into this den, Darius said, "Daniel, surely your own God, whom you serve every day, will save you." Then a stone was put over the mouth of the den, and the king sealed it with his own seal and with the seals of his nobles so that no one could rescue Daniel secretly.

The king went back to his palace. That night he did not eat or sleep. As soon as it was light, he went to the pit and called out in a trembling voice, "Daniel, servant of the living God, has your God, to whom you are so faithful, been able to save you from the lions?"

Daniel answered in a strong voice, "Long live the king! My God sent his angel to shut the lions' mouths and they have not hurt me. For God has judged me innocent and truly, King, I have done you no wrong."

The king was overjoyed and gave orders that Daniel should be brought up from the den. Then he sent for all of his accusers and they were thrown into the pit where the lions ate them, bones and all.

Then King Darius wrote to all people and nations of every language throughout the world, "May your prosperity increase! In all my royal domains people shall fear and reverence the God of Daniel, for his is a living God, a worker of wonders who has delivered Daniel from the power of the lions."

And Daniel lived and prospered in the reign of Darius.

# ESTHER

Esther 1.1-10.3.

AHASUERUS, KING OF PERSIA, ruled over an empire that stretched from India to Ethiopia. He had great power and was very rich. His palace at Susa was a maze of glittering rooms and fragrant gardens, and his wife, Queen Vashti, was renowned for her beauty.

It happened that the king summoned all of the generals, officials, ministers and governors of Persia to a great feast that went on for many days. The guests lay upon golden couches in a sheltered courtyard listening to the splashing of fountains and the music of flutes and harps. They admired the marble columns and the delicately colored mosaic floor, and they ate the most elegant foods and drank the finest wines.

The queen also gave a feast for the noble women of the court in her own richly carpeted chambers. As the women laughed and talked among themselves, servants of the king came and approached Queen Vashti.

"The king commands that you put on your royal crown and come before his guests," they said.

"Why does the king want this?" said the queen. "It is not the custom."

The servants looked at one another. What could they do but tell the truth?

"His majesty wishes his guests to see his queen's beauty," one servant answered.

The queen was displeased.

"I have become one of his possessions," she said. "I will not be displayed. Tell the king that I must attend to my own guests."

When the king heard the queen's answer he was very angry. He immediately called together his counselors to consult them about the law, for King Ahasuerus always acted according to the ancient laws of the Persians.

"The queen has not performed my command," he said. "What is to be done?"

The counselors consulted together and said, "You must add to the law a royal order that Queen Vashti may never again come into your presence. Then all Persia will know that the king's command must be obeyed, and that a wife must give honor to her husband."

This advice pleased the king and he did as the counselors advised. But when his anger cooled, he remembered Vashti and all she had done for him and he missed her. But the law of the Persians could never be changed, so Vashti went to live in a small palace with a few of her ladies and never again had to come before the king.

The king's servants saw that their master was lonely and they said, "You should seek a new wife."

The king thought that this was a very good idea. He sent out an order that all the beautiful, young, unmarried women in the kingdom should come to the palace. There they would spend a year preparing to appear before the king. He would choose a new queen from among these young women.

One servant in the palace was Mordecai, a Jew. He had a cousin called Esther, a very beautiful and wise young woman. She was an orphan and Mordecai had adopted her and raised her as his own daughter. He knew at once that Esther would be one of the young women taken into the palace and his heart trembled, for he loved her very much.

He cautioned her, "Do not tell anyone that you are my kindred or that you are one of the Jews. We came here as captives of King Nebuchadnezzar of Babylon, and though we live in every city in the Persian Empire and even work in the palace itself, we are aliens in this land. We must always be careful."

Esther promised to do as Mordecai asked but she was not afraid. She went to live in the palace. Everyone liked her, the servants because she was so kind to them and the other young women because she was so lively. She was given the best food and had the finest room in the women's quarters. Every day Mordecai walked in front of the court where the young women lived. He gossiped with the servants and heard that all was well with Esther.

For one year Esther and the other young women spent their time being made as beautiful as possible. Their skin was rubbed with oil of myrrh, their eyes were ringed with black kohl, their cheeks were rouged, they were perfumed and dressed in silk.

When the twelve months had passed, the young women were taken one by one before King Ahasuerus. But when the king saw Esther he looked no more. He loved her and set the royal crown on her head and made her his queen. He did not know that Queen Esther's foster father was one of his own servants.

One day Mordecai asked to see the queen. Esther greeted him gladly, for she sometimes missed their quiet household and Mordecai's thoughtful conversation. But Mordecai said, "I come to you on an urgent matter. In my duties I have happened to overhear two of the king's most trusted servants plotting to kill him. I have no way to make the king listen to me, but you can warn him."

"I will tell him who has done him this great service," said Queen Esther and she did. And so King Ahasuerus' life was saved by Mordecai's vigilance.

But when it came time for the king to choose one official to be above all the others in his court, he did not think of Mordecai. Instead he chose Haman. Now Haman was an Amalekite, a descendant of one of the ancient enemies of Israel, while Mordecai came from the family of Saul, the first great king of Israel.

When an order came from the king that everyone must bow before Haman, Mordecai refused. Every day when he passed Haman in the courtyards, he held his head high. All of the king's servants said to him, "If you do not obey this command trouble will come to you."

But Mordecai was stubborn and would not listen. Haman was furious but he thought that to punish one man for not bowing to him would seem petty, so he decided to destroy Mordecai by destroying all of the Jews in the Persian Empire.

He went to King Ahasuerus and said, "There is a people in your lands who do not keep the king's laws. They have their

STORIES FROM ADAM AND EVE TO EZEKIEL

own laws and live according to them. It is not right that such a people should be allowed to exist. If it pleases the king, let me issue a decree that all of these people are to be destroyed."

The king did not ask Haman what people he meant. He simply knew that he wished everyone to obey him in all things. He gave Haman his signet ring to make the decree official.

Haman wrote an edict ordering that all Jews must be killed on the thirteenth day of the twelfth month. He sealed it with the king's seal and sent it to all the provinces in the empire. Then he sat down with the king to drink wine.

But outside the palace, Susa was thrown into confusion, for there were Jews in every part of the city's life. They were craftsmen and merchants, teachers and laborers. Everywhere in the empire the Jewish people mourned. They wore rough sackcloth and put ashes on their heads as if someone had already died.

When Mordecai heard of the decree he, too, put on sack-cloth and went through the streets wailing a loud and bitter cry. He knew that Haman was taking revenge on all the Jews because of him.

Esther knew nothing of the decree, but her maids told her that Mordecai was before the palace gate wailing and dressed in sackcloth. She was puzzled and worried so she sent a servant to take him clothes and speak with him. Mordecai refused the clothes but he gave the servant a copy of the written decree.

"Tell Queen Esther that this means the death of all the Jews," he said. "Tell her that she must go to the king and entreat him to save her people."

When Esther heard this message she said to the servant, "You must tell Mordecai that if any man or woman goes to the king in his inner court without being asked, that person will be put to death unless the king holds out his golden scepter. I have not been called to the king for thirty days, and I, like anyone, may be killed for coming to him unbidden."

But Mordecai sent back this message to her, "If you do not speak to the king you will die anyway, for Haman's decree will not spare even the queen. Perhaps you have been put where you are to save your people."

Esther received this message and thought for a long time. Then she said, "Tell Mordecai to gather all the Jews in the city to hold a fast for my sake. They must not eat or drink for three days. My maids and I will fast also. Then I will go to the king, even though it is against his law. If I perish, I perish."

On the third day Esther put on her royal robes. All alone, she went into the inner court of the king's palace. King Ahasuerus was in the great hall, sitting on his throne. Esther stood quietly at the door waiting. At last he raised his eyes and saw her. He gazed at her a moment. Then he lifted his golden scepter and held it out toward her. She came close and touched the top of the scepter.

The king said, "What is it, Queen Esther? What do you want? It shall be given to you, even if it is half of my kingdom."

Esther smiled. "If it pleases the king," she said, "I ask that the king and Haman come today to a banquet I have prepared."

The king was delighted. "Bring Haman at once," he said, "so that we may do as Esther desires."

After they had feasted the king said, "I know that you must have a request of me, my queen. Tell me what it is and I swear it shall be granted."

Esther smiled. "I request that, if it pleases the king, the king and Haman will come again to a banquet that I will prepare for them tomorrow. Then I will do as the king has said and make my wish known."

Haman left the banquet feeling pleased, for he had been favored by the king and by the queen. He had enjoyed a fine banquet and had another to look forward to. Then he saw Mordecai standing at the gate. Mordecai did not bow and did not even look frightened. He simply looked at Haman. Haman was infuriated but he controlled himself and went home thinking that he would soon have revenge on Mordecai and all the Jews.

That night the king could not sleep. He asked a servant to read to him from the record of the glorious deeds and wise decisions of his reign. The servant read of how Mordecai had warned Ahasuerus about the servants who plotted to kill him.

"That was a great deed," said the king. "What honor has Mordecai been given?"

"Why, nothing has been done for him," said the servant.

When Haman came into the court the next day, King Ahasuerus said to him, "You are my adviser. What should I do for a man I wish to honor?"

Haman thought, "Who else would he wish to honor but me?" So he said, "Let this man be robed in robes the king has worn. Let him ride a horse the king has ridden and let a noble official go before him through the streets, proclaiming to everyone that this is a man honored by the king."

"It shall be done," said the king. "You shall honor Mordecai the Jew in just such a way, for he once saved the king's life." And Haman could do nothing but obey though his heart was full of anger and hate.

In the evening the king and Haman went again to the queen's palace. As they feasted the king said, "O my queen, now do you have a request that I may fulfill?"

"I have," said Esther. She went and stood before the king and looked straight into his eyes. "I ask that my life and the lives of all my people be spared. I am a Jew, one of those people who have been condemned to death by a decree issued in your name by your servant Haman."

Then King Ahasuerus turned in anger to Haman. "As you have ordered an innocent people to die, so you shall die," he said, and it was done.

"But I cannot change the edict against the Jews," the king said to Esther, "for it went out under my name and my seal."

Esther had been thinking about this, for she well knew that the laws of the Persians could not be changed. "Perhaps another law could empower the Jews to resist their fate," she said.

The king clapped his hands for his servant and called for a scribe. Then he issued a new edict saying that on the thirteenth day of the twelfth month, the Jews might take up arms and defend themselves against anyone who came to attack them. He sealed the edict with his signet ring and had it proclaimed in all the provinces and cities of the empire.

And so on the thirteenth day of the twelfth month, the Jews gathered wherever they lived to resist anyone who came to kill them. In most places they had no enemies and everyone rejoiced because no Jew must die. But where they had enemies, they fought them and killed them. And so all of Esther and Mordecai's people ended the day with thanksgiving.

King Ahasuerus made Mordecai his chief official and counselor, and Esther was his honored and beloved queen for the rest of his days.

# RETURN TO JERUSALEM

Ezekiel 37.1-14,
40.1-47.23;
Ezra 1.1-4, 6.1-7.10;
Nehemiah 2.1-7.4,
12.27-30.

MANY OF THE CHILDREN of Israel lived in exile under the rule of Babylon and then of Persia for scores of years. They were far from Jerusalem and the land that God had promised them. But because of the voices of teachers and prophets among them, they did not lose the knowledge that they were a distinct people and that they must not forget the God of Israel.

One of these voices belonged to the prophet Ezekiel. He told the people of many visions he had. He saw that the Jews had been scattered because they had not listened to God. They could listen now, he told them, and learn from the wrongs of the past. Each person had to decide to follow God, and then God would give help.

Ezekiel said, "The spirit of the Lord set me in the middle of a valley full of dry bones, and God asked me to prophesy to the bones. So I said to them, 'O dry bones, hear the word of the Lord. God will cause breath to enter you and you shall live. He will lay sinews and flesh upon you and cover you with skin, and you shall live and know that he is the Lord.'

"So I prophesied," said Ezekiel. "And I heard a rattling and the bones came together, bone to bone. Sinews and flesh and skin covered the bones but there was no breath in them.

"Then God said, 'Come from the four winds, O breath, and breathe upon these who do not live so that they will live.' Then breath came into them and they stood on their feet, a vast multitude.

"God said to me, 'These are the house of Israel. They feel that they are dead and cut off from their true place and all hope is gone. Tell them that I will put spirit within them and place them again on their own soil.'"

That was one of the visions that put heart into the people. Ezekiel also told of visions of the temple mountain in Jerusalem and the gates and walls and buildings of the temple. He saw the rededication of the temple, and he knew the laws and regulations that would be followed in the renewed Jerusalem.

So the Israelites, in exile, knew that God still had a plan for them, and that each one of them had to accept God's laws and live by them if the plan was to be fulfilled.

Under the Persian king, Cyrus, Ezekiel's prophecies began to be fulfilled. Cyrus wanted to resettle the exiles in their own land, if they chose to go. But it proved to be difficult. The city of Jerusalem was in ruins and neighboring tribes had moved into the surrounding countryside. They were not pleased when they heard that the Israelites were planning to return to Judah. There were also some Israelites who had not been taken into captivity, and they did not want to live under the rule of people who had been away for so long.

But several groups of Jews went to Jerusalem. One group at the time of Darius the First managed to rebuild the temple, and another came with the laws of Moses written down clearly. The prophet Ezra read the laws to all the people, those who had returned from exile and those who had never left, and the people began to come together in understanding. But still the city was not well defended because the walls were broken down and hostile tribes could easily attack.

News from Jerusalem came back to Persia. Nehemiah, a Jew who was cupbearer to King Artaxerxes, heard about the trouble the Israelites in Judah were having. He was very distressed.

One day the king said to him, "Why do you look so sad? I don't think you are sick so it can only be a sadness of the heart."

Nehemiah was afraid but he had to answer honestly.

"King, live forever," he said. "I am sad because my city, the place of my ancestors' graves, lies in waste. Its walls have been destroyed and its gates consumed by fire."

"You may make a request of me," said the king. "What do you want to do?"

Nehemiah was silent for a moment while he prayed to God. Then he said, "If it pleases the king, I ask that you send me to Judah, to Jerusalem, so that I may rebuild it."

"How long will you be gone?" asked the king, and the queen, who was sitting beside him, smiled.

So Nehemiah knew that his request had been granted, and he set a date when he would leave and another when he would return. And the king granted him safe passage through the province beyond the river, which lay between Persia and Judah. He also ordered that Nehemiah be given timber to be used for beams in the gates and the walls.

When Nehemiah arrived in Jerusalem he told no one why he had come. He quietly set about making an inspection of the walls so that he could plan the work that must be done. Then he called together the Jews — the priests, the nobles, the officials and the workmen — and said, "You know that Jerusalem is in trouble with its walls destroyed and its gates burnt. I come here with the support of King Artaxerxes to restore the walls and the gates."

And they said, "Let us start building."

And so they rebuilt the Sheep Gate and the Fish Gate and the Old Gate and the Valley Gate and the Dung Gate and the Fountain Gate and the Horse Gate and the Muster Gate. And they repaired the walls between the gates.

Some people began to make trouble, especially Sanballat, a Horonite, and Tobiah, an Ammonite. They did not want the Jews to grow in strength. At first they made fun of the builders but then they saw that work was progressing. The gaps in the walls were being closed, so they decided to attack and destroy the work that had been done.

Nehemiah heard about the plot and he divided the workers into two companies. One half were armed and they guarded the builders while they worked. He also ordered that all the workmen stay inside Jerusalem at night so that they would be safe.

Some people complained that the work was taking their sons away from the fields. But Nehemiah told them that he was providing food and money to those who needed it. And the work went on.

When Sanballat and Tobiah heard that the gaps in the wall

were all closed, they invited Nehemiah to a meeting in a village down on the plain. But Nehemiah was certain that they meant to do him harm so he refused to go. Four times they invited him. Four times he refused.

The fifth time Sanballat sent an open letter saying, "It is reported among the nations that you are building the wall because the Jews intend to rebel against the king. We also have heard that you wish to become king of Judah. Unless you meet with us, we will inform the king of this plot."

Nehemiah knew that Sanballat was trying to frighten him. He prayed to God for strength and sent this reply, "You are inventing these things. None of it is true."

Then Sanballat and Tobiah hired prophets to make false prophecies that would frighten Nehemiah.

"You must hide in the temple and shut the door, for they are coming to kill you," said one of them.

But Nehemiah refused to be afraid.

At last, on the twenty-fifth day of the sixth month, the wall was finished. A great ceremony of dedication took place with singing and the music of cymbals, harps and lyres. The Jews gave thanks because now people could build houses and live in the city and worship at the temple. They still had much to learn about following the ways of God, but they were a people and their chief city was again secure.

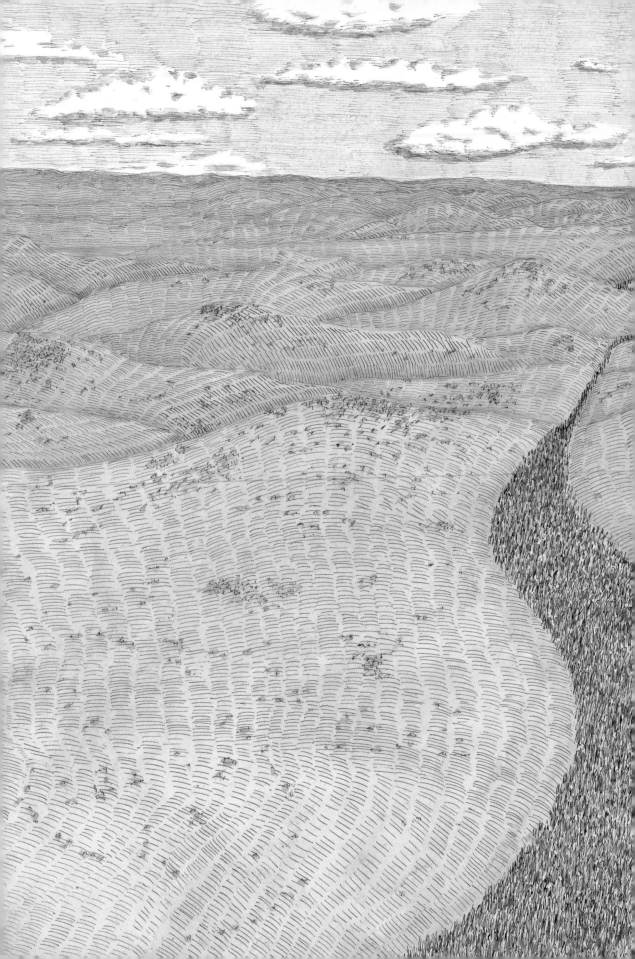